THE HEALING AWARENESS
OF MINDFULNESS
An exploration of meditation power

ISBN: 978-0-578-77337-7

MINH HAI

THE HEALING AWARENESS OF MINDFULNESS

An exploration of meditation power

ORANGE JASMINE PRESS

ACKNOWLEDGEMENT

I would like to thank Minh Ha Kasenurm for reading early drafts of my manuscript and giving me valuable insight and encouragement.

I am grateful to Ray Horn - Hanh Tri for his deep commitment to excellence and his help on reviewing the final draft.

My deep appreciation to them all. Their insights and loving-kindness is what helped fueled the many hours of work necessary to bring this book to completion.

CONTENTS

INTRODUCTION

Practicing mindfulness techniques helps to train our minds to overcome suffering. It is particularly helpful when we are faced with negative emotions that are the source of unhappiness, worry, anxiety, and so on. Having a mind predominately existing with negative emotions can bring on not only mental health issues, but it is also detrimental to physical health.

In recent years, modern neuroscientists have been interested in the miracle of mindfulness techniques and how it has been growing rapidly. They have discovered that the practice of mindfulness is to awaken the mind and body to be present in the current moment, not to be lost in day dreams, but to anticipate, and to not indulge in worries. In other words, training mindfulness is not simply a method or just a theory to read about in research papers, but it really helps the brain mechanisms retain attention and emotion. More precisely, we learn mindfulness to apply it and transform it to be a healing tool both physically and psychologically. Nowadays, many people are interested in mindfulness because this technique develops the ability to sense life deeply and to observe our experience as well.

We are living in a busy society. People can face stressors for many reasons. Maybe even at this moment someone is dealing with stress at school in the form of pressure to get better grades or do more extracurricular activities that can fill up every moment of every day. Maybe they are dealing with stress at home, in the form of financial problems, arguments, or separations. Their personal life could be riddled with difficult issues such as bullying, discrimination, poverty, family violence or community problems. Many people are dealing with chronic pain or some other chronic health condition, like diabetes. For these reasons, learning how to handle stress effectively and in a healthy way might just be the most important thing that we can do to truly thrive and reach our full potential.

The healing awareness of mindfulness explores the power of meditation. The author talks about the results of over 20 years of personal and professional experiences of learning, practicing, and teaching mindfulness meditation in Buddhism as a mindfulness teacher, practitioner, and educator. This book describes the miracle of mindfulness in educational settings for helping students and faculties reduce mental health problems. Particularly, the author also shares directly his experience about how mindfulness techniques applied in prison transfer wellness and healing techniques to prisoners facing difficult times in their lives. It is very simple, just twenty minutes of practicing mindfulness meditation two times per day can improve body and mind health.

Additionally, practicing mindfulness is the basis for awareness of community, and we can see this framework thriving in the future. When the heart is truly open, we are able to recognize what is happening around us. This has been my lifelong goal and I am incredibly grateful to have the opportunity to share my experience and ideas about the miracle of mindfulness techniques. It has the most effective interventions that work within the framework of healthcare and identify benefits to help us with mental health. In particular, the benefits of utilizing meditation as therapeutic measures in a healthcare setting have been discussed, and meditation-based interventions are increasingly being implemented adjunct or complementary to classical medical or psychological approaches.

In a busy society, many people cannot handle negative feelings and manage emotions well. Therefore, mindfulness techniques are a form of powerful medicine for people to balance their life and create happiness, relaxation, and freedom. There is no doubt about the important role of mindfulness meditation for our lives nowadays. We hope that whoever has an opportunity to read this book also becomes interested in practicing mindfulness techniques and open the door to the attainment of peace.

Orange Jasmine Press

1.

DISCOVERING MINDFULNESS

♥ What is mindfulness?

Mindfulness is originally from the East and is a popular practice in the Buddhist tradition. Today, mindfulness has been known to many people for its practical benefits. This benefit has nothing to do with the teachings of the Buddha or to become a Buddhist, but mindfulness is awakening and a sense of fullness of life; that means mindfulness can help us to be in touch with the present moment by moment with what is happening around us.

The source of mindfulness *Sati*, is from the Pāli language, and in Sanskrit language the source of mindfulness is *Smriti*, which means *to stop* and *to maintain awareness of the object*. In the Chinese character is *niàn* (念) for the word mindfulness, the top portion of character niàn (念) is Jīn (今) which means the present moment; the bottom portion of the character niàn (念) is xīn (心), which means your heart. Mindfulness is to awaken the mind and body to be present in the current moment, to be fully conscious right now and right here, not to be lost in daydreams, to anticipate, to indulgences or to worry.

Mindfulness is very convenient to practice, for you can excecute anywhere if you hold the key of practice. The energy of mindfulness is so powerful that it can help us heal our mental health. It is important to help cultivate our true wisdom and life. This is a method to help you master yourself as a real person and establish friendly relationships in your life including family members, friends, colleagues, society; furthermore, it is this world's relationship.

Mindfulness is a method that has its roots in more than 26 centuries ago and is still applicable until today.

It is suitable for Eastern society and also suitable for Western continents; in a busy society or in deserted hills because mindfulness is the awareness of the precious nature of the present moment and cultivating a friendly relationship with reality with a clear and careful attention. This attitude helps us to live more meaningful and completely different from those who take this life as something natural and very normal.

Thus, mindfulness is the essential basis of every person who needs the application anywhere and anytime. It is like a living awakening message for all of us; Not only for the disciples of the Buddha but for most people who are striving to master the mind that is difficult to control and those who earnestly desire to develop the potential of happiness, enlightenment and inner liberation of man.

Our habit is to sacrifice the present moment to find a certain happiness that has not happened, and thereby push us into a world of endless thought about a future or regrets about some past. It is difficult to separate the past and future from a human mind because people have always immersed and floated in it for a long time. The simple reason is that we do not have the ability or know how to live with the current moment. We assimilate, identify ourselves with negative emotions and think freely, and thereby creating a vision of the false ego and it has inadvertently replaced the true self inherent from one's own peaceful state.

When we are unable to live with reality, that means the mind has no place to rest, it is easy to push us straight into the world of forgetfulness, from which we are no longer aware of the connecting net between lives. Worse of all is that ignorance has led to a lack of consciousness and uncontrolled mind, affecting its actions, thoughts, and perceptions. Therefore, the connection of our life with our loved ones and the world is obstruction or become extremely limited. Living in forgetfulness is like a cut off branch of cherry blossoms, separated from the beautiful flower garden.

Mindfulness is a magical way to come into contact with the mystery of life and realize that we have a warm connection to what exists around us. When an open heart is not dominated by love, hatred, ideas, wishes, there will be new opportunities to appear, and that is the real opportunity that helps us to escape from the unconscious bondage in us.

In my experience, I would like to define mindfulness as an art of awareness living and a way to heal the wounds in the soul. We all have wounds in our minds, so everyone needs to practice mindfulness for ourselves not as a Buddhist to practice mindfulness. The most important point is that we must return to ourselves, not to become something other than ourselves. Mindfulness means observing and liberating the mind's habits of delusions of a particular self, including mental habits to evaluate things according to our interests or dislikes. When the mind has a right view that is not obscured or overshadowed by something else, that person has really seen his own nature, that is, a fully awakened person, that is a Buddha; Buddha means one who is fully awake.

Therefore, mindfulness does not carry the nuances of any religion or belief, whether it is Buddhism or science. Mindfulness is merely a way that helps us to find ourselves as we truly are through the process of self-contemplation, self-reflection, and conscious action. More importantly mindfulness helps us to return to the present moment, which is the most precious thing we inherit of life. The greatest gift that people have is the present moment, nothing else. It seems that our whole life only takes place in the present moment, and it is this present moment that helps us to overcome the confined limits of the intellect, which is the only way to overcome the tragedy of sorrow, tragedy to eradicate suffering to reach happiness and joyfulness in life.

♥ The source of mindfulness

One might think that the Buddha was the first person to teach meditation mindfulness because he was so highly praised of such great achievements. It is not at all a mystical state, beyond the reach of the average person. Yet, mindfulness manages to use these native resources to great effect to delve into the nature of suffering and the human condition. What emerged from this arduous and single-minded contemplative investigation was a series of profound insights, a comprehensive view of human nature, and a formal medicine for a treatment of its fundamental disease, typically characterized as the three poisons: greed, hatred/aversion, and ignorance/delusion/unawareness.[1] It is something quite simple and common, and very familiar to our life. In its elementary manifestation, known under the term paying attention in a particular way: on purpose, in the present moment, and non-judgmentally.[2] Mindfulness is a particular state of consciousness that involves awareness and acceptance of whatever is happening in the present moment. It is very important to think of it as fullness of mind since we bring our full, undivided attention to the present moment.[3] Attention is one of the cardinal functions of any object. If a sense object exercises a stimulus that it sufficiently strong, attention is roused in its basic form as an initial taking notice of the object as the first turning towards it. This is the reason consciousness breaks through the dark stream of subconsciousness.[4] Mindfulness is neurorestorative brain fitness designed to improve executive function. From this result we are shown that mindfulness meditation on Buddha's teachings are the rules that govern and describe the generation of the inward, first-person experiences of alleviating suffering and creating happiness in human beings. In that sense, mindfulness meditation is at its core truly universal, not exclusively Buddhist. It is neither a belief, an ideology, nor a philosophy. Rather, it is a coherent phenomenological description of the nature of mind, emotion, and suffering and its potential release, based on highly refined practices aimed at systematically training and cultivating our health, psyche, and overall quality of life.

Mindful awareness might also be noted as being about attention, and thus is also of necessity universal. Despite its Buddhist source, meditation is a secular application of mindfulness, which is a practice of carefully focusing attention. Everyone can do it, Buddhist or not, because each of the mindfulness practices mentioned above share common, secular elements: cultivating an awareness and paying attention to intention. It seems an inherent human capacity. The contribution of the Buddhist traditions has been in part to emphasize simple and effective ways to cultivate and refine this capacity and bring it to all aspects of life. In this regard, mindfulness certainly received its most explicit and systematic articulation and development within the Buddhist tradition over the past 2500 years, although its essence lies at the heart of other ancient and contemporary traditions and teachings as well, approaches that can be of great value in refining one's own practice, insight, and teaching.

Historically, mindfulness has been called the heart of Buddhist meditation.[5] Mindfulness is the fundamental attentional stance underlying all streams of Buddhist meditative practice. It came from the Buddha's traditional home, the Eastern part of ancient India. Especially, the Buddha taught the method of mindfulness in two sutras, including *Mindfulness of Breathing,*[6] *The Foundation of Mindfulnes,* [7] and many other sutras, too. After Buddha passed away, his teachings continued to rise in the Theravada tradition of the countries including Cambodia, Burma, Vietnam, and Thailand; the Mahayana school of the countries including China, Japan, Korea, and Vietnam; and the Vajrayana tradition of the country of Tibet itself, now large parts of India in the Tibetan community in exile. It should be noted that these traditions all have various schools, sub traditions, and particular texts that they revere more than others, so the actual practices and emphases regarding mindfulness can vary considerably, even within one tradition, such as a sect of Chinese Buddhism founded by the twenty-eighth Patriarch BodhiDhamma. The aim of this sect is instantaneous Enlightenment and the direct pointing at the mind for the perception of self-nature and the attainment of Buddhahood. Through vipassana or meditation on insight, meditators practice to follow the four establishments of mindfulness including the observation of the body in the body, the feeling in the feeling, the mind in the mind, and the objects of mind in the objects of the mind.[8]

Mindfulness is a direct experience of the way things are. Mindfulness is a personal journey to enlightenment, at the end of which the seeker finds he is not a person and there was no journey.[9] Mindfulness is knowing the mind, without using thought. It is living one's life by letting it live itself. Mindfulness is choosing to have no preferences. Mindfulness is becoming extraordinary by being nothing special. To understand meditation is to embrace paradox, to find the oneness that contains all opposites. We suffer from the illness of the illusion of separateness. We believe that the world is full of discrete things, when in fact it is all one interconnected whole. We experience ourselves as conscious bodies living a transitory moral life, when in fact we are the eternal mind of the universe. Separateness is the sickness and meditation is the medicine. Inherent in these definitions above is that mindfulness meditation has two key characters. The first is that mindfulness relates to the self-regulation of attention, or the ability to intentionally attend to, and be vigilant of, certain stimuli while ignoring or suppressing others. The second feature has to do with the relationship with or orientation toward experience, specifically one characterized by nonjudgment, acceptance, and inquisitiveness. The power of mindful awareness trains the brain to have focused attention and increased emotional regulation. It is being in the present moment without judgment and without attachment.

♥ Exist in the present moment

Our minds often wander after outside objects and very rarely to the present in the current moment. It is constantly drifting into the past in search of suffering or toward an unformed future project. In other words, our mind is rarely present with the body at the current time. The mind wanders through thoughts like anger, reproach, regret, anxiety, fear, sadness, etc. When you spin in this stream of consciousness, it consumes a lot of energy, it makes your life becomes disoriented and full of suffering.

These mental formations belong to the past and or the future. But the memory of the past does not exist, and the future is only a fiction until it happens. Our life is completely happening in the present moment, the present moment is the time when we really experience true life, developing or modifying anything in our lives which only is happening in the present. When your awareness is to return to the present moment, you are aware of what is happening in the body, in the mind, in feeling and in the surrounding situation. Focusing on the present moment does not mean that you are not thinking about the future or forgetting the good things of the past, but that we have an awareness that right now we are thinking about the remembering of the past, or right now, you are thinking about a project for the future.

The breath is like an object for you to call your mind back when it wanders in the past or in the future. The cause of our suffering is that the mind is always regretful of the past or worried about something in the future. When the mind exists in the present moment, which is the most peaceful state, it will create a truly free space, the present moment will develop the calm and contentment of your life.

❤ Attention with purpose

The active nature of mind is very lively, that means it runs continuingly, and is often swept away by the flow of thought that never ends. Therefore, we need a way to train the mind to stop at one place. When the mind stops, immediately it steps away from the flow of consciousness and becomes awakened. Then we have the right to put our attention to whatever place we choose. In other words, life is more conscious, alert and more complete because we control the mind, not run after the flow of the mind.

An important part of mindfulness is purposeful attention, or simpler understanding, of being aware of what is happening. When you are angry and you realize that your mind is upset, just turn on mindfulness to recognize that this anger exists in your mind. Mindfulness means gathering the mind together and towards the same object, which brings attention to the present moment.

When you are reading a book, if you are interested in the pages of the book, you will feel the messages that the author conveys in the book. Such attention may not last long, and sometimes the mind wanders elsewhere. Thanks to mindfulness you can bring your mind back to reading. Or when you eat, for example, if you do not pay attention to the food, it is impossible to know the taste of the food, although your mouth is still chewing, but in your mind you are thinking of other things, you cannot enjoy the taste of the food.

Mindfulness means only to live with the present, it's as simple as that. Most of us are always busy running around, thinking one thing after another. Can you stop all thoughts for a moment right at this moment? What will happen if you do this?

A very miraculous thing happens when you stop, immediately you will fall into the present moment. Yet present is the most wonderful state of life, suffering can only knock at your door when you think about the past or daydream about unfulfilled future. Since the past may be the sorrowful griefs that have deepened in the mind, the desire for a future that has not been fulfilled can make you frustrated. When you put yourself in the present moment, there is almost nothing that can make you suffer and hurt at all.

Thus, when you have the ability to focus your mind on a single object, pay attention to an object to experience what is going on in life, it means that you are actively reshaping the mind. In other words, you are enjoying life in a meaningful way.

♥ No judgment

Lines of unintentional thought will create a lens full of concepts, names, languages, definitions, or judgments in our mind. It forms obstacles within you and prevents you from having true views where you are and also with others. We are often dominated by these lines of thought, one after another, and then another.

Mindfulness does a cognitive job to see the workings of the mind taking place without having to control or block those lines of thought. Just do a very simple job of paying attention to the experience of how the mind is operating without having to judge right or wrong or deliberately preventing them in any form, pure identification and letting them go. That means mindfulness allows us to become a follower of the mind's flow of thoughts and emotions without being swept away by that flow. Accept whatever happens in your mind, just cautiously observe it, see the pain or joy existing, then pass and stop; whatever the form you treat it with a pure awareness.

When you have the ability to become a person who observes and follows the mind consciously, you are out of your old way of thinking and living. It really opens up a sky of freedom, true calm and happiness, and a new choice in your life begins to awaken.

Mindfulness tells us pleasant and unpleasant mental experiences without making any judgment; that means you are not governed by feelings of joy and sadness, this is called the state of equality, a balance and tranquility of mind.

♥ The benefits of practicing mindfulness in our current cultural moment

Mindfulness is a method not only important in the cultivation of the Buddhist tradition, but recently mindfulness has entered the community, practiced by many people to reduce stress, anxiety, fear, and depression in life.

Many studies have noted the practical benefits of mindfulness that can improve the physical and mental health. Some schools have applied mindfulness to teachers and students to reduce academic stress and increase tolerance and kindness in the educational environment. Many hospitals also apply mindfulness to treat patients. The prisons also teach mindfulness to prisoners so they can be calm and accepting in their situation.

Thanks to the widely published scientific research in the media, mindfulness is no longer confined to traditional Buddhist monasteries or stored in ancient library texts. Today mindfulness is benefited by millions of people around the world. As the masses continue to explore the incredible benefits of applying mindfulness to life, their interest continues to soar over time.

Practicing mindfulness with the right instructions will bring changes in your mind and gradually achieve lasting happiness. For the sake of mindfulness is not merely to calm the body and mind while practicing, but it also positively affects underlying brain patterns such as awareness of anxiety, stress, depression, and anger. When they arise, they will easily disappear. People who practice mindfulness have improved memory, increased creativity, their responses have been more agile and they are less likely to see a doctor than the average person.

Anyone can practice conscious breathing. If you continue to practice, your mind will not be distracted, you can practice like for ten minutes twice a day, and after a week you will see change in mind and body.

Mindfulness is you returning to yourself. We often get caught up in our daily work, emails, answering phone calls, and so on. Our mind always flies along hundreds of thousands of objects and rarely abides in ourselves. Such living seems to become a habit and increasingly we become alienated to ourselves, the connection between body and mind is really out of touch. It is an alienation phenomenon which is very common in society today. Conscious breathing is an effective means to bring us back to ourselves. This return can be made with an extraordinary speed without waiting in line to buy a ticket. Returning to the breath means you are returning to reality here and now, done quickly in an instant. Relying on the breath to return to yourself, you have a great feeling of peace and serenity. That experience is like a son going back to his ancestral home. This home gives you the warmth and it is here that you find yourself. Is returning to yourself a great success of cultivation? The Great Beings are returning to themselves to understand and find who they truly are.

Mindfulness is being exposed to the fact that life is already here. We can only meet with the present moment. If we are not exposed to the present moment, we cannot contact life. Our whole life only happens in the present moment. If you want to be in touch with the present moment, you have to have a peaceful, gentle peace, that is, the mind is always present with the body, not attached to past regrets or worry about the future. When you return to the present and you have mindfulness, that is truly the best moment of life. Nature is so wonderful that life is miraculous. If we are bound, how can we be exposed to that mystery, that is, we cannot really live our lives? Returning to conscious breathing is one of the miracles to get rid of the constraints and we can immediately come into contact with the present moment. Just by focusing on the breath, all the burdens of suffering in us suddenly disappear, giving way to a strong, quiet but lucid consciousness of reality. In that state of clear consciousness, what is needed for the moment naturally appears itself.

Mindfulness calls you to take place to touch and embrace in the present moment. Most of us cannot live in the present moment. Our mind is always focused on the memories of what happened in the past or anticipation of the dream in the future. We usually keep the mind focused on anything but what is happening around us in the here and now. This is why we become caught up in a way that hijacks our attention, making it more difficult to stay in the everyday moments of our life. Touching life can help you to recognize how to be more alive and make life more valid for you. In this way, you and your beloved both receive nourishment. Imagine that you are practicing mindful drinking while drinking cup tea at early morning. If you are being here in the present moment, which is nothing short of a miracle, the tea reveals itself to you. You will also reveal yourself. This is drinking tea in mindfulness. You are already touchment life, and your life is deeply in the present moment.

Mindfulness may strengthen and train. Practicing mindful awareness by the following the breath can be compared to muscle-strengthening techniques. As with all muscle training, our mindfulness can be strengthened when we frequently exercise. In contrast, our muscles weaken or atrophy when we do not make use of them. The miracle of mindfulness is similar to the program training of the muscle, strengthening mindful awareness as we practice.

Mindfulness might cultivate. To practice mindful breath, we might take great care in the garden of our life, watering and caring for our mind. Aware that everything nourishes our garden mind, including the positive influences on our lives as well as the negative ones. The difficult influences in particular, what one mindfulness meditator has called the compost of our lives,[10] can provide a rich source of nourishment for the wonderful flower, which is the art of living that we learn to meet with practicing mindful of the breath.

Mindfulness applies to training your capacity for nonjudgmental awareness. To practice mindful awareness breath shows us how caught up we are in judgments, ideas, and opinions about things and our lives in general. The result of mindfulness meditation may be that it is possible to set judging aside and experience elements of our lives in a less-filtered way, free of tunnel vision. This way in turn creates a richer and clearer understanding that we have a choice about things. Opting to exercise that choice becomes a conscious step toward mindful action, rather than a detour into wishful thinking, resignation, or impulsive behavior.

Mindfulness gives you access to your own insight. To practice mindful breath is to discover that innermost awareness pervades every moment of consciousness, including every single thought. It is not possible to bring out innermost awareness in its nakedness without being introduced to it first, because it is bound and obscured by conceptual thinking. Using mindfulness gives us access to the rich ground of wisdom, insight, and compassion in our lives.[11]

Mindfulness gives you access to your own concentration. Sometimes the flowers are so beauty in the grarden, but you did not see them. When you are mindful and concentrated, you can say, "I see you". You see the flowers that you had not seen before. The miracle of seeing happens when you are mindful and concentrated within your own, and you can see and listen to everything deeply, and the fruits are always understanding, love, acceptance, and the desire to relieve suffering and bring peace. Mindfulness is the course of peace.

Mindfulness gives you access to your own compassion. Compassion has to do with particular qualities of attention and awareness that can be cultivated and developed through mindfulness. Researchers shows the reduction of stress in health care workers and providing self compassion through practicing mindfulness technique.[12] Our health is easy vulnerable to stress overload and compassion fatigue due to an emotionally exhausting environment. Praciting mindfulness helps us wake up from this sleep of automaticity and unconsciousness, thereby making it possible for us to live our lives with access to the full spectrum of our conscious and unconsciousness possibilities.[13] It helps you to hold thoughts, emotions, feelings, and see your surroundings in every moment, then you can come back to yourself with compassion and take a good care your life. It is the continuous practice of touching life deeply in every moment of daily life. To be mindful is to be truly alive, present, and at one with those around you and with what you are doing.[14]

Mindfulness gives you access to your own freedom. Touching freedom only happens when you are free from narrow views and abtain fearlessness, more mindfulness and concentration. Sitting on the cushion and watching your breath in and out is a wonderful practice, but it may be not enough. For healing and transformation to take place, you should be practiceing mindfulness all day long, everywhere and everytime. Your mind has a habit to never stop thinking. You lose yourself in the past or worry about the future, and sometimes you get caugh in your fears or anger. That's the reason why you do not have your own freedom. When you are practicing mindfulness, you are in contact with life, and you will offer your kindness, compassion, and love, which is the power of mindfulness to lessen the suffering and bring about happiness and freedom.

Assume someone is engaged in a hazardous activity such as climbing up a mountain or balancing on a highwire. While the activity is happening, the athlete is focusing on the present moment. Her or his mind state is only being here with the game. They do nothing else, without thinking of other times or worrying about any of the heavy burdens placed on his or her shoulders. Because they really know that if they are not focusing on the present moment in each second, they may be unable to face the danger that exists. Playing such hazardous games provides an opportunity to come back to current times. To practice mindfulness technique, you can touch and pay attention in here and now without needing to engage in the danger of climbing a rocky mountain. All you need is to come back to your breath and follow that breath in and out with full awareness. You and the breath are one. Then you are relaxed, joyful, and without the worry, fear, anxiety, or desire that has wanted to control your mind. Practicing mindfulness technique really helps you lead a happier, deeper, healthy life, transforming and healing pains, and bringing forth peace and liberation.

Mindfulness is a miraculous method that helps us to stop thinking, judge and control all activities of the mind, approaching the present moment with a warm and peaceful experience to ourselves and others around us. When we master the method of mindfulness, wherever we go in this world, we still have peace in us and this can help us to return to where we are, what we are doing. feeling and clearly seeing everything.

We can apply mindfulness in our daily work, not waiting for an internship in the monastery hall. Sit back and relax, come back to the breath. Practice like that for a few minutes, then we feel good. Take our steps, step by step leisurely, so that each step in every breath, listening to the wind, birds singing, crickets, we will feel strangely peaceful.

The power of mindfulness provides a range of rich resources for personal practice and dialogue with psychotherapy that might contribute toward the training and development of a cohort of highly competent teachers. The result and benefit of mindfulness comes from a wide variety of professional backgrounds, committed to the effective delivery of authentic mindfulness-based interventions in various settings.

Mindfulness is often spoken of synonymously as insight meditation, which means looking deeply and engaging in penetrative non-conceptual seeing into the nature of mind and world. Most people are forgetful, they are not really there a lot of the time. Their mind is caught in worry, fear, anger, and regret. They are not mindful of being there. That state of being is called forgetfulness, which means we are there but we are not there. When our mind loses mindfulness, the eyes look at things, but we do not see; the ears hear sound but do not know; the mouth is eating but does not know the taste of food.

Mindfulness is when you are truly there, mind and body together. This seeing requires a spirit of perpetual and persistent inquiry such as, what is this? toward whatever arises in awareness, and toward who is attending, who is seeing, who is meditating. When our mind is there with our body, we are established in the present moment. Then we can recognize the feelings that might help us move toward a healing and transformation of metal health. The role of mindfulness in deep inquiry and the cultivation of insight have led some to argue that that mindfulness provides a unique perspective that can inform critical issues in cognitive science, neurophenomenology, and attempts to understand the cognitive underpinnings of the nature of human experience itself.[15]

Thus, mindfulness is an art of living in awareness. Anyone can practice and inherit the practical benefits. But the most important thing is that we know how to apply it, that is, stop all thoughts to go back inside. When we really come back inside, we will realize our true nature, then all difficulties and miseries pain will be metabolized and treated.

2.

BREATHE TO HEAL
AND TRANSFORM

Practicing mindfulness meditation has the power to bring the mind back to the body. If we want to be as close as possible to an object that is constantly present and direct to us, it is the breath. The breath is the perfect and most effective choice for practicing mindfulness meditation. The Buddha also used his breath to practice. Nowadays meditators also use this method to introduce and teach meditation in many meditation centers. Because the breath is something specific, it is always present in our being. It has the function of maintaining attention so that we can relate directly to the functioning of the five factors that make people, called the five universal mental formations, which include form (material element of the body), feeling, perception, mental formation, and consciousness (the mind). When you consciously focus on the breath, it is an easy way to recognize the movement of the mind and clearly identify changes in the body.

The breath is an object for the mind to dwell on and to make mindfulness arise. The breath is very easy for the mind to rest on because it is always with us, does not cause annoyance, does not cause any pressure, and does not bind us. With the breath as object, we can experience it directly without the intervention of thought or any existing experience. Because the breath is a living reality, when we return to the breath, we also return to the living reality of the present moment. Therefore, we choose it as the source for the mind, discovering the functioning of the mind.

The breath is a natural process. You do not need the will to interfere because the breath still takes place as rhythmically as usual in its own way. Therefore, when choosing the breath as the object of the mind to dwell on while practicing mindfulness, we also need to respect its innate nature. That is, we perceive the breath in and out, long or short, consciously, without the attitude of interfering or forcing it to be this or that.

Following the breath metaphor for a gate keeper, he did not check each and every person when they came in and out of the city, nor ask who they were, where they came from, and what they had in their hands. Because these are not his duties, he does not care about the details of each person. His task is to sit there to see each and every one as they enter and exit at the gate. Similarly, the breath when entering or exiting the body is not of the practitioner's concern. The practitioner is aware only when it passes through the touch point within the range between the tip of the nose and the top of the upper lip.[1]

In the Mindfulness of Breathing,[2] the Buddha introduces us to the methods of practicing the breath in a very simple, specific, and clear manner. If we learn and practice, we can transform stress, anxiety, fear, lust, hatred, and despair. We sequentially learn the sixteen exercises of mindfulness breath presented in an essential way as told by the teaching of the Buddha.

♥ Aware of breath

"Breathing in a long breath, I know I am breathing
in a long breath.
Breathing out a long breath, I know I am breathing
out a long breath."[3]

The breath is the first choice of meditators when practicing mindfulness meditation, because the breath is a means of familiarizing and reconciling with the body. We sometimes breathe without paying attention to the breath completely. So, the purpose of this exercise is to identify conscious breaths. While I breath in a long breath, I know this is a long breath and when I breath out a long breath, I know it is a long breath. Beginners starting this practice of mindfulness meditation can find that it takes time to pay attention to the breath. When the mind follows the in-out breath, that makes us stop thinking.

Practicing like this after a few breaths, the mind will settle into the in-out breath, and we don't need to be repetitive like a machine, but we should let the conscious breath carry the breath in-out naturally. Of course, we only have a bare attention of the breath without the attitude that makes the breath lengthen or short, merely bare attention observing consciously. While breathing it is possible for the mind to generate thoughts, which disturb our consciousness. When that happens, you should not repel or suppress these thoughts, but let the mind know it and return to the breath. The mindful breath helps us to stop the stream of thoughts, then the mind immediately calms down and is physically present.

Everyone breathes, but we are rarely aware of the breath, so the body is here, and the mind runs away elsewhere. Therefore, we are not really present in the present moment and are not exposed to the wonders of life. The first breathing exercise helps us bring our mind back to the body, to be present with the present moment. We can only enjoy life in a profound way when the body and mind are present now and here. In life you can apply this exercise whenever and wherever. Just by consciously monitoring the in-out breath, the mind immediately returns to the body, which is the gift of life to all of us.

♥ Following in your breath

"Breathing in a short breath, I know I am breathing in a short breath.
Breathing out a short breath, I know I am breathing out a short breath."[4]

Practicing mindfulness by following the breath from beginning to end, following naturally, without any experience's intervention. I am breathing in to know that I am breathing in. Let the mind be completely rested where the breath is not interrupted, so that concentration will arise. By focusing on the conscious breath and resting on the in and out from the beginning to the end, mindfulness and concentration are deeply present and the presence in the present moment is one of more solidarity.

If you practice breathing in – out and following your breath completely, then you feel light, peaceful, and happy. The pleasure and joy gained in practicing breathing will give you a wonderful life experience, that you are still alive, and all lightly undulating thoughts naturally stop. Because our minds for so long have been thinking about many things, indifferent to the breath, we do not feel the miracle of the breath. That said, it does not mean that your mind is completely pure or free of disturbing emotions, but that through practicing breath awareness you can identify the emotions there, without repulsion, and without trying, calm them down. In the practice of mindfulness meditation, we are practicing being aware of all the phenomena that are happening in the mind, and to avoid the attitude of repelling, coercing, and repressing what we don't like. If you try to control your breath, pitting ideas of wholesome versus unwholesome, it is like turning your consciousness into a battlefield, and sitting there receiving bombs and bullets is very wasteful.

Practicing the second exercise of following your breath helps you to be continuously present, uninterrupted, and we can come in contact with the mystery of life. Many times in our life, we are here and our mind is elsewhere; so the ancients said, "If the mind is not here with the body, then even if I look with my eyes I cannot see, though I have my ears and not hear, even if I eat, but don't know the taste of food."[5] If the mind is not here with the body, then we are like a dead person. When the mind truly returns to the body, then we can truly live a life worth living.

♥ Aware of whole body

"Breathing in, I am aware of my whole body.
Breathing out, I am aware of my whole body. He or
she practices like this."[6]

Practicing aware of breathing helps you to be mindful at every moment in your life. The power of mindfulness helps you know what is being released in the body, which is the meaning of this third exercise. Breathing in I am aware of my whole body, breathing out I am present with my whole body. The breath is the gateway to help us return to reunite body and mind. The more you practice the more deeply you feel and recognize the amazing mystery of the breath.

We have few opportunities to look deeply and understand the hardships of our body parts, so many times we have treated them with little attention and made them miserable. Smoking and putting alcohol into your body cause damage to your lungs and liver. Worry, sadness, and anger make the heart work harder and the blood vessels weaken, causing serious illnesses. Mindfully breathing helps you to contact each part of the body, understand their functions and tasks. From there you realize how to live with good behavior that is not hurting the body. When you know how to love and comfort your body, you will be able to love others.

More importantly, when we are physically present, we are able to detect and discover in our body a number of illnesses such as aches, fatigue, stress, anxiety, etc. That it can have from being compressed, abandoned, or superficially treated. For a long time, we are proud of our body as a spiritual temple, but we only know how to apply lipstick, shoes, and outer clothes. We have never listened to what our body needs and the difficulties it is facing. Thanks to the breath awareness, you bring your mind back to your body to see the aches and tension in the body, the source of all kinds of illnesses.

♥ Let relax of the whole body

"Breathing in, I calm my whole body
Breathing out, I calm my whole body. He or she
practices like this."[7]

When it is discovered that the body has stress and aches, if left untreated, it can generate many diseases for both body and mind. Breathing in, I calm my whole body, breathing out, I calm my whole body. A peaceful whole body means relaxion of the whole body, that is, letting the figure become calm, letting tension, pain, and fatigue come out of the body. A robust body has a lot of energy and a bright spirit. Therefore, the mindful breath has miraculous healing and preventive power.

You can practice letting go of your body while you practice walking, standing, lying down, and sitting down in mindfulness. The mindfulness teachers recommend that we practice lying down before going to sleep, lying comfortably on the muscles in our body, returning to the breath, watching the breath going in and out, helping us let go of fatigue, stress, anxiety after a long day of working or studying. Practicing like this helps you have a good and deep sleep without any nightmares in your sleep, because all the stress in your body and your head has been calmed and released.

Practicing step-by-step relaxation, also known as walking meditation, is also a capable means of eliminating anxiety and stress. Taking aware and mindful steps, we will see a lot of happiness in every step. Walking mindfully like this gives the whole body the ability to let go of many burdens and cure many ailments. Each of these steps of mindfulness can remove the burden of sorrow in your heart, helping you to miraculously connect with life, which is a miracle of mindfulness.

♥ Joyful creation

"Breathing in, I feel joyful.
Breathing out, I feel joyful. He or she practices like this."[8]

Meditators often look at their bodies as a river. The river is created from many drops of water. There are many cells in the body, each cell has a different function to perform in the body. Every minute, cells die, and new cells are produced. The body is a living entity like the flow of a river. Our feeling is like a flowing waterfall.

Our feeling is sometimes calm, gentle, and sometimes intense and uncomfortable, but it still silently flows night and day without interruption. Each feeling is based on the immediate environment and the surrounding environment. Breathing in, I feel joyful, breathing out, I feel joyful. This exercise helps us to touch and come in contact with what is fresh and clear and has metabolic and therapeutic properties. It may have been that for a long time we have been trapped in a prison of grief, sorrow, or despair, and we have had no chance to come in contact with freshness, so sometimes in our mind there is an invisible wall separating us from the outside world.

We are not directly contacting by senses the things we are contemplating. We can only contact through images that already exist in the mind, called the object-domain of mere illusion. This is one of the storehouse consciousness seeds that can wake up when you invite it. When the freshness is awakened then you will begin to be nourished again, your life becomes beautiful and worth living.

♥ Create happiness

"Breathing in, I feel happy.
Breathing out, I feel happy. He or she practices like this."[9]

Mindfulness meditation has the ability to help you create the material of happiness and peace. Happiness is something that must be created; it is not automatically available. Happiness and peace are two very important qualities in the process of practice. They are a strong foundation to help us make progress on our spiritual path and also to nourish us with intense vitality. Breathing in, I feel happy, breathing out, I feel peace. This is not a selfish desire for one's self, because the Buddha always encourages his disciples to manipulate joy, freshness, peace, and happiness in the life of practice. The practice of mindfulness meditation does not need to be desirable to become enlightened or to become a Buddha, but we can experience fun and happiness while practicing. If we practice mindfulness meditation without fun, then why practice? Therefore, you need to learn how to create a peaceful and happy energy during your practice to grow the energy of concentration and insight.

Joy and bliss come from getting away or leaving something behind, which means letting things go to create happiness and peace. For example, someone tells you something hurtful, and you keep it in your heart, and every time you think about it you do not sleep well. With the practice of mindfulness, you can realize whether or not that hurtful experience is worth making you so sad. Why would you confine yourself within a sentence that still makes your soul wither and torments your heart? Mindfulness can wake you up and give you the ability to let go of that burden, and joy is immediately present.

Joy and bliss come from right mindfulness. The power of mindfulness helps you to truly exist in the present. The breath has the energy to bring the mind back to the body and help us to realize that we are still living fully with every moment of our life, which is the greatest gift. There is no guarantee you will go up to the moon with oxygen to breathe, with green trees, and hearing the birds singing by the hills. Awakening to this, we cherish life, cherish loved ones, and cherish what we have. Thanks to mindfulness, we are grateful, and the grateful person is a happy person.

Joy and bliss come from right concentration. When there is mindfulness then right concentration is present. When you are aware of a cup of aromatic tea in the morning, it is due to mindfulness. But you can maintain that presence longer thanks to right concentration. Right concentration is born from right mindfulness. While drinking tea and experiencing the joy in the taste of tea, you have a lot of happiness. Thus, the longer one holds the concentration, the greater the mindfulness and more peace of happiness.

Joy and bliss come from right insight. Wisdom or insight is a clear and transparent view. When faced with a problem, if you have strong mindfulness and attentiveness, you have a very clear view. Because the power of insight helps you talk, act, think clearly, and treat others well, so as not to cause suffering to yourself and others. That transparent view is a gift of true joy in life to you.

❤ Identify pain

"Breathing in, I am aware of my mental formations. Breathing out, I am aware of my mental formations. He or she practices like this."[10]

Mindfulness in breathing helps us to realize the pain in our body. This exercise helps many people identify *internal fetters* of the past that cannot be erased between themselves and their families or any relationships that have been fostered from childhood. The wounds of an unhappy childhood, such as one involving domestic violence, makes them not want to think about their loved ones. Because the sorrow and resentment are always inside them, it is very painful to face it, and even creates nightmares.

In the first step, we visualize our self as a vulnerable boy or girl, when we were severely punished by a stern eye, a scold, or disrespectful disregard, leading to sadness and guilt. We feel very pitiful and sorrowful. In the next step we smile at that susceptible person, that child who is us, with compassion and loving-kindness from a merciful heart. The third step is to visualize the person that tormented you as a vulnerable girl or boy, and to realize that they were also the victim of the same wounding treatment from others in their past.

Thanks to the power of mindfulness and concentration you can get to know, smile at, and be friendly with the vulnerable boy or girl, be it you or them. There is a sense of generosity and forgiveness rising in you when that compassion flows out of the heart. It is then that the signs of therapy and transformation have begun. Looking deeply into the root of the matter with understanding, allowing love to be present, the inner circle will transform, and forgiveness will begin to be accepted. Practicing this firmly will not only transform and treat the pain but also be able to help others transform. We believe in this because our understanding and love have transformed us and we become fresh, sweet, gentle, serene, calm, and patient. Mindfulness helps us to be calm and patient. Calmness is a sign of the transformation of suffering and patience is the true sign of love.

❤ Be accepting of pain

"Breathing in, I calm my mental formations. Breathing out, I calm my mental formations. He or she practices like this."[11]

When you have so much peace and happiness, the ability to accept and forgive is very easy. The practice of mindfulness meditation does not seek to flee from pain, nor does it seek to cover or suppress pain. The meditator's attitude is to be able to face pain directly when he or she discovers that they are present, and then accept the pain to seek treatment and transform them.

Breathing in, I know there is a pain in my heart. That pain needs to be cuddled and recognized. "Dear pain! I know you are there. I will not run away from you." We need to have the courage to accept the existence of the pain and use mindfulness energy to embrace that pain, even though we have not done anything to reduce our suffering.

A handful of salt poured into a river will not turn the river into a body of saltwater. But if you pour that same handful of salt into a glass of water, you will have salty water. In the same way, our mind has the tolerance and acceptance that is just as full as the river, and a handful of frustrating salt, or two or three, will not make us suffer. On the contrary, if our heart has little compassion, just a small unpleasant occurrence can also make the heart feel tormented. The mindful breath has the ability to nurture and expand the compassionate heart. When the compassionate heart is huge, it is possible to take care of, protect, and accept the suffering and unfortunate events. It is a miracle of mindfulness meditation practice.

♥ Aware of mental formations

"Breathing in, I am aware of my mind.
Breathing out, I am aware of my mind. He or she
practices like this."[12]

The purpose of this exercise is to recognize and name mental formations with intension whenever they appear. The mind works like a river in which fifty-one mental formations[13] are operating without stop at extraordinary speed. The mind manifests and connects with each of these formations like a river. Looking at a river, you get the impression that the river is an entity that doesn't change, but with careful observation you can see that the river is always changing. It was Heraclitus who said that you could not step twice into the same river because different water is always flowing past you.

The mental formations manifest very quickly and continuously. Sometimes we have the feeling that consciousness is something that lasts forever. The mind-stream is like a cinematographic mechanism of the mind.[14] As in watching a movie, we have the feeling that it is a story that happens continuously, but in reality, it is a director's arrangement, the sophisticated techniques of the producers connecting each scene individually into a movie. Consciousness is also a series of arising and passing away, or birth and death, in every moment, and it is the nature of the seeds that create those mental formations.

We practice mindful breathing to recognize when the activities of mental formations arise, such as sadness, anger, happiness, etc. Our task is to observe the ongoing mind formations without clinging to them, nor dispelling them, whether they are positive or negative mental states. When we control our mind and our emotions, we are a free person.

♥ For joyful mind

"Breathing in, I make my mind happy.
Breathing out, I make my mind happy. He or she
practices like this."[15]

The purpose of this exercise is to make the mind happy and peaceful, which is a vital energy needed to nurture the practice, that is, the practice of identifying and caring for the mind. Within, we have holy and pure mindful traits such as generosity, tolerance, forgiveness, etc... So, in the process of practicing how to water those traits, you yourself become holy, and that is a big step on the path of practice.

The task of practicing mindfulness meditation is to take care of the mind. When the mind flies around here and there, we have the task of awareness to invite the mind to lie quiet. When the mind is calm, positive energies easily arise, which is a necessary condition for cultivating peace and happiness in our life.

Practicing meditation is also known as a method of training the mind or improving it. Mind itself has very noble qualities, so we must diligently clean and dust away the disturbing emotions that may be clinging for many years. When our mind is enlightened, we have the ability to know the mind's movements. The important thing here is to choose the right one, to bring comfort, then continue to invite that quality.... that is the happy mind.

♥ Concentrate the mind

"Breathing in, I concentrate my mind.
Breathing out, I concentrate my mind. He or she
practices like this."[16]

We all have made mistakes, caused crashes and injuries to ourselves and others. Those clumsy mistakes are often due to wrong perception, such as feeling afraid of the rope because we thought it is was a snake, a simple delusion. People suffer due to false perceptions by imagining things that are not real.

Suffering can go on and on when we don't have the right mindfulness to recognize a wrong perception, not only hurting ourselves but also others. More dangerous, we do not know how to transform the injury, but just blame the situation on environment, condemning this person and blaming the other, which never solves the problem.

With mindfulness, the right understanding, and the right view, we can see that the root of suffering is created by us. How many mistakes are also caused by our mind. With that right view, we no longer blame others, but we find the real reason and the determination to revise it by being mindful while thinking, being mindful while speaking, and being mindful while acting. On that basis, we can bring joy to ourselves and not cause others to suffer right now. Then peace will follow. That is the result of this exercise.

♥ Liberation free of mind

"Breathing in, I liberate my mind.
Breathing out, I liberate my mind. He or she
practices like this.[17]

Our mind is always bound by ropes of hatred, animosity, and despair. These ropes make us suffer. Thanks to mindfulness and concentration we can eliminate the wandering thoughts and suspend the sensation of a life surrendered into oblivion. The energy of concentration and mindfulness can burn those ropes and untie our mind from attachments, thus liberating the mind.

When we put our entire mind on the breath, the mind only follows the breath; the mind with the breath becomes one, which is called concentration. This liberating concentration occurs when the contemplative subject and the contemplative object become one. Concentration is the state of stopping the mind from converging on a single object. Only we ourselves have the ability to contemplate and open up the traits in our mind. Just like when we want to remove a tangle of knots, we must have enough time and relaxation to do so. Contemplating the mind for calmness and depth we can remove the trouble from our mind. This is an important step in mindfulness meditation practice. We can do this entirely by using conscious breath monitoring and breathing.

♥ Contemplating impermanence

"Breathing in, I observe the impermanent nature of all Dhammas.
Breathing out, I observe the impermanent nature of all Dhammas. He or she practices like this."[18]

The mindful breath will help us to have an impermanent view of all Dhammas. When we look at the development of the body, we see it always changes like a stream that keeps flowing. Through that image, we will see the nature of impermanence and transformation of the body. Looking at a picture of when we were five or seven years old compared to the picture of when we are thirty, we see we are completely different. There's nothing the same, the shape, the feeling, the thoughts, the actions, and the consciousness, and yet we are still the name Jenifer, or Steven. Our names are still the same, however our physical growth and mental formations have caused a change in us.

We suffer because we do not accept that all phenomena change. The mind is bound to a person we love, and it is unbearable when we have to leave them. The truth tells us that human beings or living beings that have existed for a while will eventually be destroyed. Suffering is created because we are not able to realize and accept that law. If we have peace of mind we will not suffer as much.

Because we are not aware of the impermanence, we become weak minded and unkind to the person that we love. We are tortured if someone does something wrong to us. If we know our beloved person is impermanent, then today we can do something to bring happiness to them instead of blaming them for our anger. If we can do anything generous, then do it today. Do not wait until tomorrow. Because tomorrow we may no longer have the opportunity to do so. Therefore, impermanent contemplation brings a lot of happiness for us and for our loved ones.

♥ Contemplation of not being greedy

"Breathing in, I observe the disappearance of desire. Breathing out, I observe the disappearance of desire. He or she practices like this."[19]

Greed is one of the causes of insecurity and grief. Mindfulness helps you realize what is worth pursuing, what is worth keeping. There are many people who identify themselves by the compliments of others. But if those compliments are removed, they feel empty and devastated. When we are able to calm down, one thing we realize is that the more indulged we are in chasing after material things, the less able we are to find peace. Being absorbed with such greed actually destroys peace.

Not knowing when we have become passionate about high-end technologies to serve our own comfort endangers us to be immersed in them to the point where we lose our right to life. Time for work takes up all our daily activities, and after a long day of work it seems like we have no strength to enjoy our self. So busy we are that there is no time to take care of our health, no time to see our loved ones. In the beginning, there were always projects based on others, so we did not have the conditions to learn life experiences, and did not have the patience to listen and understand our children, parents, and family members. More dangerous is that the constantly developing greed in our mind negatively affects the moral qualities and wholesome qualities of life.

When we contemplate ways of not being greedy, we know how to stop in order to lead a life for ourselves, be successful, and also have happiness. Not being greedy doesn't mean you have to give up everything or avoid it in order to find a safe existence. Instead, you know what is enough to live, not chasing after unnecessary things, having time to look after ourselves and others. In truth, a person is happy when he or she knows when enough is enough. People who are greedy still feel poor even though they may be living in a palace.

♥ No birth, no death, looking deeply

"Breathing in, I observe the no-birth, no-death nature of all phenomena.
Breathing out, I observe the no-birth, no-death nature of all phenomena. He or she practices like this."[20]

Birth and death are an interesting contemplative topic in the teachings of Buddhism. On the relative side, we see that everything comes and goes, there is birth and death, there is loss, there is gain. But the insight of the Buddha shows us that all things are no birth no death, no being no nonbeing, no defilement no purity, no increasing no decreasing.[21] Zen masters often give examples of clouds to know the non-arising and non-death. The cloud is not from nothing in becoming something. Before it became a cloud, it was the water of the ocean, and thanks to the sun's heat, the water evaporated, and thus climbed up to meet the cold air thus condensing into clouds. The presence of clouds is just a continuation of heat and water. Clouds can only become snow, become rain, become fog, become ice, clouds cannot become nothingness. So the cloud is not nothing but becoming something, the cloud is just a continuation, its nature is no birth and no death.

The nature of humans, including the Buddha and even us too, are no birth no death. In the practice of mindfulness, we contemplate deeply into the world of phenomena in which we discover no-birth no-death nature and enter the world of nature. The process is going from the mark (laksama) to the nature (svabhava), from the sign to the essence.[22] When it comes into contact with its nature, it is exposed to its nature which is called no birth and no death. No birth or death represents the eight mental complications, which include neither birth nor death; neither permanence nor end; neither identity nor difference; neither coming nor going.

When we see the nature of all Dhammas and our nature is not birth-not death, then we are fearless and no longer greedy, and we will gain fearlessness. Without fear, happiness is truly perfect. As long as there is fear, then that happiness is not perfect. Moreover, seeing the nature of no birth and no death, it is possible to ride on the waves of birth and death, go on, and smile with all the waves that come, no longer afraid of death, no longer afraid of birth, because birth and death are just an idea.

♥ Contemplation of letting go

*"Breathing in, I observe letting go.
Breathing out, I observe letting go. He or she
practices like this."[23]*

What is worthy for us is to let go, which is to let go of the notions of *birth – death; end – permanence; identity – difference; coming – going*. We must let go of all these notions; let go of the *neither birth nor death*, because the nature of phenomena of *birth – death*, is that nothing appears, nothing disappears, which means there is neither origination nor cessation; refuting the idea of appearing or birth by the idea of disappearance. Let go of the *neither end nor permanence*; because the nature of phenomena of *end – permanence*, is nothing has an end, nothing is eternal, which means neither permanence nor permanence; refuting the idea of permanence by the idea of destruction. Let go of the *neither identity nor difference*, because the nature of phenomena of *identity – difference*, is nothing is identical with itself, nor is there anything differentiated, which means neither unity nor diversity. To refute the idea of unity by the idea of diversity. Let go of the *neither coming nor going*, because the nature of phenomena of *coming – going*, is nothing comes, nothing goes. To refute the idea of disappearance by the idea of coming, which means neither coming-in nor going-out, refuting the idea of coming by the idea of going. These are the eight mental complications.

The reason we suffer is because we are afraid, and we grieve over ideas. Time is a continuous flowing river, but because you have an idea of time, you choose a point in that time, as when you are born, so then you have to die. So, there is a certain point called death. Then from the notion of birth – death, we have the idea of a life span of a human life. We can live 60 years or 100 years. From there I think that before I was born I didn't have this life, I only had it from the time of birth and it would end when I died, meaning that we are non-existent then we exist, then nothing again, so that is why there is the idea: yes – no; before – after; birth – death that causes us suffering and misery.

It is the mindful breath that makes it possible for you to let go of all those thoughts. When you let go, you become a person without fear and become a free, happy person. It is the happiness that comes from practicing with mindfulness and insight. The Buddha taught that all of us can practice being able to let go and achieve that true happiness.

Although the breath has its origin in the mind, it is still called a bodily-formation, which is a physical artifact.[24] The mindful breath is an energy that anyone can create in himself. This energy is capable of helping us truly be fully present in the present moment, the true mind uniting with the body. We can apply mindfulness to everyday while sitting, studying, working, to make our lives more qualified and valuable. Mindfulness as the secure mind has the power to protect, enlighten, nourish, love, transform, and heal us, because the nature of mindfulness transports itself in the energy of right concentration and wisdom. When you breathe consciously, mindfulness is present, there is concentration and insight. With mindfulness and insight come the intention to lead, your life is always peaceful and happy. The greater the concentration and wisdom, the greater the awareness of mindfulness. Consequently, mindful islands are the safest and most secure refuge. Come back to true refuge in the island of self-awareness, never relying on any other object.

Many people in our society are faced with stress, depression, anxiety, and loss of peace. They must take tranquilizers such as *trifluoperazine, antidepressants,* to help the mind rest. But the medicine only helps a certain part, they still experience the dreamy layers of suffering such as anxiety, fear, anger, and torture. The stressful work, the accumulated schoolwork, makes the mind think too much, which is why you lose energy, spirit, and have headaches. The monitoring of the breath and the coordination of conscious breathing creates the security to help us transform and treat the mind's endless stream of thoughts. The sixteen exercises of mindfulness of breath presented above light the torch of awakening. You do not need to practice all sixteen exercises at once, nor do you need to practice the order from one to sixteen. Just understand the use of each lesson and apply a few exercises that you feel at peace with during your practice. Breathing in and out consciously is a very miraculous practice that has great metabolic and therapeutic properties, and anyone can do it.

3.

THE WAY
OF MINDFULNESS

The heart of Buddhism is mindfulness meditation. Practicing mindfulness meditation is turning back toward the inside. If we want to stop the mind from running around then the mind must be stopped – in the meditation called *samatha,* which is stopping, calming, letting go, concentrating and cooling the body and mind; and looking deep, called *vipassana*, which means deep looking. Mindfulness meditation calms the mind, enabling it to let go, and then contemplate its nature to see the roots. In other words, mindfulness is stopping all thoughts to be present in the present moment and looking deeply into reality to see what they are. Therefore, mindfulness is meditation and meditation is mindfulness, so we can practice mindfulness wherever and whenever. We can practice mindfulness daily. When we are walking with awareness of our breath and our steps, this is called mindfulness while we are walking, when we eat while being aware that we are eating, it is called mindfulness while eating, and so it is with other activities. If you practice like that, you really bring meditation into life.

Pausing and resting is a very simple, practical, and important practice for living in today's busy society. We have a habit of wandering and seeking happiness from the outside. So many lives have been passed on like this, now we continue roaming, even while sleeping. We have a faith and an idea that happiness is only touched in the future, so we seem to have sacrificed all the time in the present to search for happiness in the future. Meanwhile, the Buddha taught that we can only live happily in the present, not in the past nor in the future. If we stop to establish a solid body and mind and stop wandering, seeking, and grasping, there will be plenty of ways to have happiness in life.

The Buddha taught that all Dhammas are created by the idealistic thought process, that is, all phenomena of things are created by our mind. If our mind is full of insecurity, anxiety, and sadness, how can we be happy and peaceful? Therefore, if we want to have peace, Buddha taught us to go back to our true home to understand and see clearly the changes of our mind.

♥ The path of transformation

There are many methods that Buddha gave us to practice to transform the mind. Mindfulness is one of the most effective methods of mind training because mindfulness instructs us to do everything we need to do with complete awareness. Why is full awakening important for our lives? Everyone can recognize that when the mind and body are present for each other, the more attentive they become to actions, feelings, thoughts, and perceptions. These become more apparent and we are aware of what we are doing. Awareness helps us see actions rooted in the motive of good or unwholesome, the mind of compassion, tolerance, and generosity or anger, ignorance and indulgence. When mindfulness is present, it will help us to stop and identify just like that, then we know what we need to do.

In *The Foundation of Mindfulness*,[1] the Buddha talks about the four observations, including the observation of the body in the body, the observation of feeling in feeling, the observation of mind in mind, and the observation on objects of mind in object of mind. With these four contemplative headings, the Buddha teaches us to practice insight, to include the whole person and the whole range of human experience. They range from the body and its functions to sensations from the process and content of awareness and reflection. The method of mindfulness helps us begin to embrace the shape with the awakened energy and the practice of contemplation from the earliest beginnings to the absolute greatness of this complex human being. These include ordinary human functions such as breathing, eating, excreting, up to the higher levels of the element of freedom, happiness, peace, and liberation. There is a most wonderful way to help living beings realize purification, directly overcome grief and sorrow, end pain and anxiety, travel the right path, and realize nirvana. This way is the four establishments of mindfulness.[2]

Mindfulness technique is a very interesting practice process that helps us to interact, explore and contemplate, to see the true nature of reality in a direct way – called bare attention.[3] Bare attention, or pure identification, is to keep the mind pure and simple on what happens to us and inside us at continuous moments of awareness. That is to give a sense of what is happening with the body, sensations, mind, and objects of the mind, without thinking about judging why there is pain, why there is sadness, why the mind is insecure. The more we think, the more miserable we are, the more energy we lose, and the lesser the facts are. When focusing on an object and merely recording the observed events without interfering with any action, language, or explanation, it can be interpreted as an expression of attitude, favoritism, or hatred of judgment or inference. If, for a long or short period of time, we maintain a state of concentration for bare attention, and, if the concepts of renunciation or love arise, we recognize them, then we will not be chasing those mental states.

♥ The observation of the body in the body

Focusing on the breath is the best way to start practicing mindfulness meditation. The breath is the most readily available and constant tool in the body. Just coming back to the conscious breath is connecting the body to the mind immediately. The breath is a vital source of life because every part of the body needs the action of the breath to provide oxygen with the breath in and out. Everyone has experience with breathing and just by paying attention on the breath, mindfulness is present.

Not only human beings breathe, but all animals breathe too. Breathing is not just for those who follow Buddhism, but also those who have other religious or non-religious traditions must also breathe. People in the East or the West, upstream, midstream, or downstream also share the same breath. Although we have been and will be breathing all our lives, we are rarely paying attention to the breath and never know what is really going on with the breath. The practice of focusing on the breath is fundamental and indispensable to creating peace of mind and spiritual progress. Therefore, the Buddha advised us to begin to contemplate the breath in order to understand the contemplation of body contemplation.

♥ Mindfulness of breathing

This step is beginning to contemplate the body in the body by focusing on the in and out breath with the principle of simple bare attention. This means focusing on the beginning, middle, and end of each in and out breath. Awareness throughout the breath cycle is called mindfulness of breathing. When the mind is present at the breath, the mind is no longer wandering, and the body will relax. This is achieved when the body, mind, and breath are relaxed.

Experiencing the body with attention through the breath, rather than conscious breathing exercises, this method does not mean we hold the breath or extend or shorten it. We are only using bare attention to merely observe the naturally occurring flow of the breath with a firm and sustained attention, with ease, without tension or rigidity. Long or short breaths are noted but there is no interference by anything else involved in the process of breathing in or out. There are some Zen masters who recommend focusing on the up and down movement of the abdomen to monitor the breathing in and out. You will find the abdomen rising when you breathe in and falling when you breathe out. The rising should be noted mentally as *rising*, and the falling as *falling*.[4]

Practicing calmly, quietly, and deeply breathing in and out, tranquility will naturally form and that is an important factor for physical and mental health. When we relax our muscles, we feel better after five or ten minutes of practice. Mindfulness of breathing helps overcome obstacles such as insecurity and drowsiness. When our mind is deeply conditioned, there is joy and freshness. This is very natural because when there is relaxation in the body, the mind is also relaxed, because the breath is a part of the body and mind. When the mind merges with the breath, the mind does not get caught up in the emotions of greed and fear but becomes peaceful and serene. With mindfulness of the breath in and the mindfulness of the breath out, you will have happiness, a natural birthright.

The mindful breath is very helpful for yourself and for everyday activities. Practice the habit to practice a few breaths before making important decisions, such as talking, signing on responsibilities, or dealing with some exciting cases. You will maintain a calm attitude and avoid agitated language or actions. By simply observing the breath, we immediately become mindful, remaining comfortably with awareness, relaxing into the events as they occur right in front of us and right in the present moment, not focusing on the habits of anger, resentment, or fear. Mastering emotions with mindfulness, we realize that the only place we can find peace and freedom from suffering is the present moment in our body and mind. In this way, mindfulness is helping people become perfect for themselves.

Mindfulness on the breath will increase the overall understanding of the true nature of the body, because the breath is identified with the life force itself.[5] Watching the breath come in from the beginning to the end completely also helps us to realize the impermanence of the body. Pay simple attention to any pains in your hands, shoulders, or back, as well as any relaxation in your body. We have been neglecting listening to the body for so long that we have abandoned it. When there is joy or tension, just recognize and smile at them. It is a method of renewing us and we become fresh and pleasant, and seeing these things is also fresh and soothing.

♥ Mindfulness of the bodily posture

The activity of the human brain occurs naturally and automatically with the human body. The nerves automatically connect to each other smoothly without any control. The heart also pumps blood without any prompting. The practice of mindfulness of the breath also needs to occur continuously in order to recognize the postures of walking, standing, lying, sitting, sleeping, waking, talking, or being silent, and he or she also shines that clear consciousness into himself. The body is giving oxygen continuously to sustain life.

In everyday life we rarely have the opportunity or do not want to fully observe the postures of the body. The practice of mindfulness in the movements brings very practical benefits in life. Being mindful step by step gives the mind the opportunity to become aware, and all the hasty impulses in the nerves involved in brain function will be trained to become calmer. Other postures such as standing, lying down, sitting, sleeping, waking, talking, and silence, can be enlightened by mindfulness so that unnecessary and damaging postures will be avoided. When the body is cared for, it avoids futile fatigue, and the mind also becomes relaxed.

It is important to focus on the postures of the body as it is necessary to have a conscious contemplation of the gestures of the operation of each part of the body to understand and have a chance to make deeper contact with the body. Mastering your body in all situations, being aware of all movements and actions helps them become more rhythmic and at peak performance. More importantly, having mindfulness of body postures is not only to observe the details of movement in the body, but also to give us the opportunity to observe what is going on in the mind; through movements in our steps we can train the mind.

♥ Clear comprehension extends to all functions of the body

Mindfulness of the body's parts is focused on monitoring every part of the body including visible parts such as skin, flesh, nails, etc., and invisible parts like bones, liver, bile, etc. These parts are tied to us but sometimes we forget. Every day they work hard to support this body, but we never pay attention. Sometimes they protest because of tiredness, aches and pains, but we ignore it. Because in our daily lives we are often occupied by work. The mind, immersed in thousands of thousands of objects, jumping from one object to another, becomes habituated and has little chance of returning to itself. Mindfulness helps the mind return to the body to recognize parts of the body; it is a return to the root to restore the human integrity that has long wandered around. Life that can become miraculous is rooted in a state of mind and body.

If there is mindfulness to contemplate this body, it is not at all a monolithic solidity, but it consists of many combined elements of thirty-two parts. Of these, twenty solid parts include hair on the head, body hair, nails, teeth, skin, flesh, tendons, bones, marrow, kidneys, heart, liver, spleen, chest, large intestine, small intestine, undigested food, stool, and brain. Twelve liquid parts include bile, sputum, drool, pus, blood, sweat, fat, tears, saliva, mucus, oily water in joints, and urine.[6]

Mindfulness of the body's parts opens the mind to a way of seeing and accepting itself as it is, not having a passionate reaction to being beautiful and not being disgusted when there is something unsatisfactory. This helps us to overcome the complacent or hateful habits, enabling us to see the body with our equal mind. An analogy could be a bag containing a mixture of grains like brown rice, pearl barley, buckwheat, mung beans, speckled kidney bean, black soybeans, oatmeal, pea, small red beans, black glutinous rice, corn, and husked lotus. A person who has bright aware eyes when looking at those nuts, recognizes them; these are brown rice, pearl barley, buckwheat, mung beans, etc., merely recognizing the name. He doesn't need to be discriminating by saying he likes brown rice or hates black glutinous rice.

The method of mindfulness meditation on parts of the body, as stated in the text by the Buddha, advises us to merely identify. By practicing this we can develop love and cherish our life. Moreover, when we look deeply into every part of our body, we see the predestined nature of birth carrying a message of truth about the nature of the universe. Each hair is filled with the whole universe, and the universe is in a single atom.[7]

♥ The observation of the feelings in the feelings

Feeling in Pāli language, is *vedana*. In Buddhist psychology, feeling has three states: pleasant, unpleasant, or indifferent sensation. They come from physical or psychological elements. In this sense, feeling is the first reaction to all thoughts and emotions, so those who want to control emotions need to learn how to master feeling. In the dependent origination doctrine, it is said that all human feelings originate from the conditions of sensation. Deep inside, feeling is the quality of craving, and even worse, clinging.[8]

Feeling is the crucial point, the doorway, in the arising of suffering, because it is in feeling that arises the different emotions, the joys or sufferings that come from this feeling. Mindfulness meditation helps you recognize and master the sensation to break that feeling. Practicing mindful breathing is an opportunity to recognize feelings at the very first level when they begin to manifest. Just by giving a mere attitude of recognition, you will find their roots. As you wake up this morning, you have the unpleasant sensation associated with fatigue, headache, and frowning. Contemplating that feeling you see that it is the result of a lack of sleep because of staying up late to watch movies last night. Feeling in this case is rooted in the physical. Or when you are misunderstood, out of anger or jealousy, and you have frustrating feelings, this kind of feeling has psychological origin. When you are aware of those feelings, breathe and tell them: "Hey man, you are annoyed! I know you are in me! Hey jealous sister, I know you're in me!" You can smile at those feelings.

We often have habits in the mind of greed arising when there is a pleasant feeling, hate and anger when faced with an unpleasant sensation, and a tendency to ignore when there is a neutral sensation – uncomfortable and unpleasant. It seems that we have such reactions, but we all know how that pleasant feeling can satisfy our greedy mind. Unpleasant sensations that we don't ask for, but just silently come to us as a natural occurrence in the rules of life, no one can escape. Running away from neutral feelings is also a foolish act. Thus, craving for a pleasant feeling is greed; hating the unpleasant feeling is anger; and avoiding being neutral is delusion. Greed, anger, and delusion are the root of all suffering. Mindfulness of feeling is an opportunity for us to identify the source of suffering, then we can let them go gently.

Practicing sensation mindfulness is a simple and non-judgmental way of identifying what we are experiencing. According to this formula when you contemplate a feeling of joy or sadness or unhappiness it is not sad in that feeling itself, this feeling is not mine or a part of my ego. Observe each sensation when it arises, be present, and it will disappear, and give an awareness that every feeling always changes, coming and going, and is impermanent. Pleasant sensations do not last long, unpleasant sensations often cause suffering; they are all unsatisfactory. Attention is merely a feeling in the body or an emotion of the mind, rather than a feeling of mine. We will come to realize that feeling is also not self. The truth of realizing feelings as they truly are must be practiced and applied in each of our lives.

Carrying the human condition, everyone has feelings of joy and sadness, each experience is suffering or happiness physically and mentally. Pain and fatigue from work, loneliness and sadness from being separated from loved ones, depression because of adultery, everyone in life has more or less had these experiences, because life does not give us all. However, practicing mindfulness in feeling will help you master these emotions. You are no longer chasing emotions of sadness, blame, anger, and jealousy. You have truly returned to yourself, back to the pure nature, which the Buddha called the Original form or Buddha nature, a very beautiful nature that has existed for a long time, but forgotten because of being filled with greed, anger, and delusion from the sensations that lead us that way.

♥ The observation of the mind in the mind

Within the mind is the mental phenomena sometimes called mind or mental formations (skt: citta-samskara). *The Foundation of Mindfulness*[9] lists the types of mental formations, such as attachment, hatred, ignorance, gathering, distraction, generosity, finite, supreme, concentration, and liberation. The mind is the objects of contemplation of the mind in the mind. The mind does not stay in your body, or stay outside of body, or stay in the center of your body. You can not find the mind in your body, or out of your body, or in the center your body. The mind is very hard to see.[10] It does not stay in a particular place, so it is said that the mind does not dwell anywhere.[11]

But the mind is in fact a series of moments in a very small unit of time, interconnected with the mind in the mind. The practice of mindfulness helps us to know that the mind arises continuously in every moment of the shortest period, according to information from external senses such as seeing, hearing, smelling, tasting, and touching, and with the inner state of mind such as ideas, imagination, memories, and delusion.

Most people avoid looking directly at the mind, perhaps for fear of seeing their own shortcomings or having those shortcomings disturb the complacency of the ego inherent in each person. If a mistake is discovered, then as an instinct, people find every way to cover up for that mistake. Such an attitude of running away will make us helpless to prevent the unwholesome cittas from appearing.

The light of mindfulness is lit to reflect on our mind, we don't just look at the mind. The essence of the mind does not exist alone, but the mind always exists according to the external and inner conditions, that is, when the six basics are in contact with the six mortal beings. By focusing on the way every thought arises, is then present, and then vanishes, we gain the valuable experience of stopping the unsatisfactory thoughts that are always jumping from one thing to another. In this way, we let go of the wandering thoughts and understand that we are not those thoughts. After a while, we come to know what it truly is.

♥ The observations of the objects of mind in the objects of mind

This method relates to the mind and the object of the mind, which is the dhamma. Dhamma here means the content of thinking. Contemplating on the doctrine to experience reality and attain freedom and happiness. Human suffering comes from wrong perceptions. Despaired because there is no proper view of the nature of reality, or in other words, there is no right view. The breath of mindfulness is capable of giving a correct view of the phenomenal nature and discovering the causes of suffering and fear. Practicing insight into reality needs to be thought of in everyday life.

Here, the Dhamma that Buddha encouraged us to contemplate includes 1 / the five principal mental hindrances; 2 / the five aggregates of clinging; 3 / the six sense spheres; 4 the seven factors of awakening; 5 / the Four Noble truths.

❤ The five principal mental hindrances

Nibbana that we merely need to know exist in the mind are desire, aversion, sloth and torpor, worry and restlessness, and doubt or uncertainty. They are presence or absence, arising or not arising.

❤ The five aggregates of clinging

Khandhas, which is materiality, feelings, perceptions, mental formations, and consciousness arising or falling away. Knowing these and dwelling in awakening we will not fall into the attachment of these aggregates.

❤ Mindfulness of the six sense spheres

Ayatana consists of the six internal senses; the eye, the ear, the nose, the tongue, the body, the mind when exposed to the six outer forms of sights, sounds, odors, tastes, tactile sensations, mind objects. The six consciousness consists of sight consciousness, hearing consciousness, scent consciousness, taste consciousness, body consciousness, and mind consciousness. All phenomena are contained in eighteen categories, the Buddhist term called the eighteen brahma worlds, which contains three components: psychological, physiological, and physical. All are mental objects that we call the mind of dhamma. When the mind contemplates the mind, the mind also becomes the object of mind.

❤ The seven factors of awakening including mindfulness

It is investigation of dhammas, energy, joy, ease, concentration, and letting go. The person who practices mindfulness concentrates the mind to know that the factors of enlightenment are present or absent, arising or falling away. The person who lives contemplating the arising and passing-away of phenomena dwells in contemplation towards mindfulness. If practice is like that, he or she does not depend on nor is attached to anything in the world.

♥ The four noble truths

Teaching that when the fact is suffering, he or she contemplates: this is suffering. When events are the cause of suffering, he or she contemplates: this is the cause of suffering. When the fact that suffering can be stopped, he or she contemplates: suffering can be stopped. When the fact is the path leading to the end of suffering, he or she contemplates: there is a path leading to the end of suffering.[12]

The quintessential teaching of Buddhism are these four noble truths. Buddha confirmed the presence of suffering, but at the same time demonstrated the presence of happiness and nirvana, affirming the ability to transform suffering to happiness. Metabolism of suffering will be present. The two sufferings (dukkha) and habits (samudaya) describe the state of reality as suffering and its causes. The next two truths are the end (Nirodha) and the direction (magga), which describe the ideal state and the three. The hope is for us to step forward. The truth of Suffering is contrasted with the truth of Cessation, that is, happiness exists in the absence of suffering; The truth about suffering is contrasted with the truth about the way, the path of Dhamma practice leading to the suppression of suffering when seeing their cause. The path of practicing the teachings to end suffering is right understanding, right thinking, right speech, right action, right livelihood, right effort, mindfulness, and concentration, these are the eight righteous paths that lead to happiness.

When practicing mindfulness meditation on *the Foundation of Mindfulness*, the Buddha advised us to apply a bare attention method that is to look within the body, feeling, mind, and all Dhamma methods to recognize what is happening to us. Seeing the tired body, unpleasant sensations, and the mind of greed, just keep on noting those phenomena that are present, then they will disappear. Also, when you see a healthy body, feeling joyful, happy mind, you also notice that they are present, and then disappear.

Mindfulness of the process of a phenomenon which arises, appears, and disappears, will help us to realize that phenomena are impermanent, that is, detect, existing and disintegrating according to the dependent origination law. The Buddha taught, "This is, because this is. This is not, because this is not. This is produced, because this is produced. This is destroyed, because this is destroyed."[13] According to this principle, all Dhammas cannot arise, exist, and cease alone, but the arising, existence, and annihilation of one Dhamma are based on other dhammas. Dhammas do not arise, exist, and perish on their own, so the Buddha taught that dhammas do not have a separate entity, so they are sometimes called empty. Emptiness here just means there is no entity, no separate entity.[14] The dhamma is simply phenomena, and contemplation on the object of dhammas leads to the understanding that a phenomenon is both impermanent and non-egoistic.

The negative habits or practices of akusala citta (unwholesome mind/thought) always bind us to attachment, insecurity, and suffering. The binding mind is like the shackles that lock people down. By practicing efforts, you will remove the habits of greed, anger, delusion, and ego. Thus, the four forces of contemplation are a very direct method, able to eliminate the habits of akusala body and mind, and nurture good qualities based on the correct understanding of Buddha. When the shackles are finally broken, we gain freedom, liberation from all suffering.

Of course, you don't need to practice all the foundation of mindfulness at once. Understand the meaning of each field of mindfulness and apply it to the object as needed. There are some people who practice mindfulness meditation to reduce stress, fatigue, and bring good health to the body and mind. But practicing mindfulness meditation in the four areas of mindfulness achieves even more benefits.

Mindfulness meditation helps you to be awake and recognize what is happening in the body and mind at the present moment. Mindfulness meditation is a bridge between body and mind, you are no longer worried about the past or daydreaming about the future, you are truly an awakened person. In other words, by practicing mindfulness, the fog is cut and the meaning of life becomes real.

Mindfulness helps us assess the purpose and appropriateness of all actions, words, and thoughts. It helps us avoid mistakes for ourselves and for others and results in more wise and beneficial choices than before.

Mindfulness helps us to see our true body, feelings, and thoughts as they are in each moment. Observing the process of arising, surviving, and disappearing of a phenomenon that occurs in the mind is a fundamental step for us to make positive changes to life.

Our life becomes profound and meaningful if we practice mindfulness and apply it to our daily life.

When the mind is clear, we look at the world around us properly, without distortion.

Practicing mindfulness helps us become more calm, deep, and see the world around us in a true way without distortion. We come to the predestine understanding that everything that exists, including all sentient beings, both good and bad people, are interrelated and interdependent, no one thing exists separately, and everything always changes. Therefore, we understand there is nothing, no-self, no material, or circumstance that can exist forever and perfectly.

Mindfulness shows us through life that life is a dissatisfaction, but not a complete suffering, if we can transform the mind to be happy. Dissatisfaction is a fact, and it is possible to have peace if we know how to transform our mind.

Thus, if you practice the correct method of meditation with confidence and diligence, the enlightenment that the Buddha teaches will have the power to quell suffering and lead to the path of peaceful happiness, peaking in liberation, nirvana.

The conclusion is that mindfulness meditation trains your mind to stay awake, think, speak, and act with awareness. More specifically, with this new enlightenment, you begin to realize that everything in life is impermanent, the essence of each natural phenomenon has no self. Because the nature of all phenomena changes without hesitation, and our thoughts and emotions are always flowing as the river. The awareness of everything that appears and disappears in a flash like a morning dew in the grass, is a lesson for us to step out of this craving, this stubbornness that is ours. The enlightenment of impermanence and non-self will remove the mistakes that seem fixed and immutable, then you are able to escape suffering.

The way of mindfulness has a powerful and noble function. Anyone who practices this methodically will be happy. It is a gift from the Buddha the blessed one left for us. Every day we practice mindfulness, we receive the valuable gift, which is life.

4.

THE BRAIN DURING PRACTICING MINDFULNESS

Mindfulness meditation is like a jewel for today's human civilization. Human spiritual life will greatly reduce stress, anxiety, and depression if mindfulness meditation is incorporated into daily life. Westerners from the mid-20th century began to study and practice mindfulness meditation, especially young people and the intellectual class. Because they feel that material comforts are not enough to make happiness, the sorrowful and depressing worries in life can only be answered by the method of spiritual life. Mindfulness meditation in the Buddhist tradition is capable of contracting with the spirit of science, cooperating with science in the field of discovering spiritual truths and dealing with people's suffering psychologies.

Scientists have studied mindfulness meditation and discovered its benefits in treating illnesses arising from people's minds such as depression, anxiety, fear, and depression. The material of compassion, tranquility, kindness, and care enhance the quality of life giving yourself and others a gentle freshness. The practice of mindfulness meditation has a nourishing and therapeutic effect on the body and mind, bringing a source of joy to the practitioner. Results of of brain studies conducted while practicing mindfulness show changes that certainly related to changing moods and emotional states in people.

♥ The operation of brain waves

The human mind shows a close connection with the energy and information that occurs in the body. These include the brain and the relationship, the dimension of the mind relative to the flow of energy and information that occurs between people and situations. For example, when I sit down to type these words, the mind is immediately connected with my hands on the keyboard in a harmonious way, the mind is with me at this moment.

One of the most important organs that has direct and indirect contact with the mind is the brain. The human brain weighs about three pounds, or 1.36 kilograms. But inside the brain is 1.1 trillion cells, including one hundred billion neurons. On average, each neuron receives about five thousand contacts of information from other neurons, called synapses.[1] The brain is an extremely complex mechanism for it leads to our ability to think, remember and understand emotions and to plan behavior. Understanding some of the basics of how the brain works can provide an insight into how the brain creates and how it reflects our states of consciousness

The combination of synchronized electrical activity in the brain is called the brain wave, because of its cyclic nature like the wave-like wave. Brainwaves can be detected by a medical device, such as an electroencephalogram (EEG), which measures fluctuations in electrical levels on different areas of the scalp. These measurements tell us about the various internal functions of the brain. Brain waves are divided into five different waves that are said to create a universal human consciousness. Although divided into five different waves, each layer of brainwaves change throughout daily life, due to being influenced by what we are doing, thinking and our emotions at any time, even while sleeping.

The brainwave bands consist of simple brainwave bands that are frequently clustered into groups based on their shape and function. There are several levels of brain waves:

♥ Delta waves

Delta brain waves range from 0 hertz to 4 hertz cycles per second and are considered the slowest brainwaves humans can produce. It has the advantage of resting the brain and increasing creativity.[2] They are usually produced during the deep stages of sleep (stages 3 and 4) and are involved in regulating unconscious body processes such as regulating heart rate, kidney activity and digestive function.

Delta waves are typically generated in the right hemisphere of the brain and are linked to our subconscious and unconscious processes. Young children tend to have uniform delta activity, but as we age the delta activity becomes increasingly sparse, even during sleep. While you are in a state of uniform functioning, you are not consciously aware. Delta brain waves help the body heal and can release various hormones including human growth hormone (HGH) at different frequencies. It is linked to the unconscious mind, which means that the reaction is uncontrollably conscious. The bodily functions are unconsciously regulated including heart rate, breathing, kidney function, digestion, deep sleep, enhanced immune system function, and increased empathy, etc. All unconsciously conditioned processes involve delta activity. We can also see increased delta activity in damaged brain regions in some way. Once again, this is how the brain closes down everything for rest and healing.

♥ Theta waves

The Theta wave is faster than the delta's active frequency, but is still slow, usually running between 4 and 7 hertz cycles per second. Theta waves are often associated with relaxation, meditation practice, intuition, and higher consciousness.

Theta waves are often associated with subconscious. There is a lot of research that shows that theta waves have a positive impact on people's mental health, like lower stress levels, clearer thinking, an enhanced creative intelligence and more.

Theta waves have powerful stress relieving properties. When the brain is in a state of high Theta production, we get calm, relaxed, free from stress or anxiety. If you want to encourage a calm and balanced state, practice meditation and live a relaxing life.

♥ Alpha waves

The frequency of the Alpha brainwave ranges from 9 to 14 hertz cycles per second. Alpha represents the stimulus, it is in neutral position, the speed is medium. Alpha often involves relaxation and inner focus.[3] Such a person has completed a task and sat down to rest often in alpha state. You take the time to ponder or meditate often in the alpha state. Or you take a break at a seminar and take a walk outside the park, usually in alpha. When the eye is open, we receive a lot of external images and the brain is dominated by that image. At this time the ability of alpha brain waves is low. But when the eyes are closed, the outside contact is closed, and the stimulation impacting the brain is reduced. Therefore, when you close your eyes, the possibility of alpha brain waves is very high.

♥ Beta waves

The range of beta waves ranges from 16 to 30 hertz, and usually has a high amplitude. Beta brain waves mainly occur when we are alert and performing a task involving positive thinking. Beta waves are associated with the conscious mind. When a person practices mindfulness meditation, and acquires concentration while walking, sitting, or doing any other work in life, the beta brain waves do not appear. Beta waves appear quickly and are associated with many activities. When we see an increase in beta waves when a person is involved in activities such as projects, thoughts, worries, etc. This is the brainwave that we want to go in to balance schoolwork or occupational work. It doesn't really help when we want to rest or make good sleep.

♥ Gamma waves

Gamma waves oscillate rapidly and are often found during conscious cognition. They are usually at the top of the range that you will see in any study of brain training. The increase in gamma waves is associated with very sharp focus and a sense of creativity, intelligence, and energy. An explosion of gamma brainwave frequencies is often seen during high levels of information processing or when different components of the brain work together to integrate information. Unlike the process of beta, active gamma brain waves usually involve effort and want to be understood.

A brief summary of how the brainwave activity works can help us see clearly and understanding why fluctuations are so different in the brainwaves can give us a basic understanding of how the brain works. We need to practice mindfulness to transform when external circumstances affect our minds. If we are not flexible, it will affect our mental health.

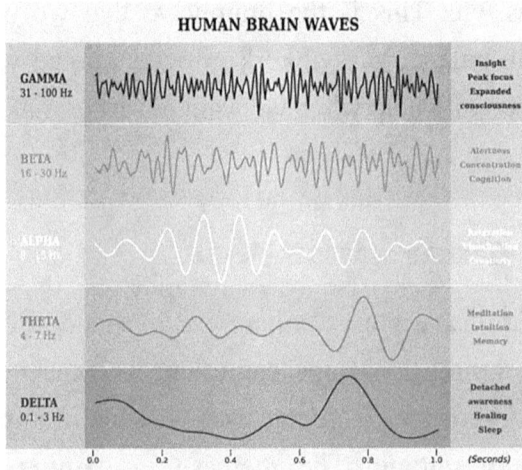

HUMAN BRAIN WAVES

Research shows that when one practices mindfulness meditation, one can see an increase in Alpha waves on the back of the head, an increase in Theta in the anterior region, and an increase in Gamma on the left in the anterior region.[4] This influence is due to the effect of mindfulness meditation practice, when the brain is trained by mindfulness to cause all brainwaves to pass through equitably and improve positive feelings like happiness, peace, ans calm.

❤ Our brains while mindful meditating

Many interesting studies on the benefits of mindfulness meditation show that it does have a positive effect on the brain. During meditation practice, there are states in our brain that are focused attention, open awareness, and automatic self-transcending.[5] Practicing mindfulness meditation also increases lovingkindness and compassion. Mindfulness in the general sense is awakening the inherent potential of awareness from the natural and sensitive life of recognizing new things in everyday experiences. With mindfulness awareness and the flow of energy and information received by the mind into conscious attention, we can evaluate the content standard and also adjust its flow in a new way. Conscious mindfulness, as we will see, is really related to many things, not simply cognition: it involves awareness of aspects of the mind itself. Instead of being automatic and not thinking, mindfulness helps us to awaken, and by thinking about the mind, we are enabled to perceive and make choices and thus change becomes feasible.[6] The brain neurologists show us that when applying meditation to watch and observe, the brain has four types of states that can be found when practicing mindfulness meditation, including:

Mindful awareness, which is the state only for open monitoring, which involves innocence, impartiality, non-judgmental evaluation, and only actual contact with reality awareness.

Quiet mind, which describes the state as automatic self-transcending, which is the goal towards the superior healing of mindfulness meditation practice.

Pay attention, which is like concentration or focused attention, and is related to intentional control and clear awareness.

Open heart, sometimes called lovingkindness and compassion, which is a form of practice involving the initiation of a positive or willing idea or feeling. Dedication to help others with warm hearts.

♥ Mindful awareness

The energy of mindfulness helps us to do everything we need to do with complete awareness. It really helps us to live in such a state of joy, peace, and happiness that sometimes they just drift through our lives without us being aware of it.

No matter how strong and satisfied the concentration is, it is impossible to be complete without mindfulness to support and deepen the concentration. If there is only concentration, then this state has a tendency to hide like withdrawing from the world around it. The typical energy of concentration is closure, withdrawal, and deep sleep, which lack the energy of observation, openness, and awakening. When we come into contact with any phenomenon experienced by humans that is capable of perceiving all of these, it is the use of mindful awareness.

Mindfulness has the power of liberation because it helps us to truly live with ourselves and with what is happening around us. Mindfulness takes you out of the deep, deep pit of forgetfulness. Moreover, mindfulness can empower us and give us strength, because it helps us unlock the stored energy of creativity, intelligence, imagination, determination, knowing a choice and a hidden insight in us.[7]

Studies show that when measured by electroencephalogram (EEG) for people practicing mindfulness there is an increase in strength and connection in front of the Theta brainwave.[8] Mindfulness is being aware of all thoughts and awareness of what you are doing. Sometimes you start to focus on something you are doing, that mindfulness is maintained for a while, and then we will do it unconsciously. The fall back to this habit of ignorance sometimes stems from the cause that what is happening is not attractive, so the mind wants to find something else that is more interesting; sometimes what next is more attractive, and our mindfulness practice is not big enough, so it is difficult to cultivate mindfulness in the long run.

You can reflect to see the habit of the mind which is always wanting to hide the present moment. Close your eyes right now, return to the in – out breath, watch the in – out breath, the belly bulges out, the belly expands. You discover that in order to maintain mindfulness you must be awake and conscious. We practice this by always reminding ourselves to be mindful while doing anything. Just like that moment from moment to moment, from job to job in daily life, you have a wonderful peace. The great effect of mindfulness practice can improve self-monitoring and executive aptitude related to self-awareness. Thus, mindfulness is an effective remedy for ADHD recovery, it is also suitable to heal wounds like cravings, and slowly change harmful habits, lifestyles, and addictions.

In addition, practicing mindfulness is also beneficial for healing anxiety. Mindfulness helps Theta brainwaves become stronger, making anxiety not existing anymore.[9] This is not surprising, as the brainwave increases in front of Theta during meditation, reducing the level of anxiety.[10] Another study also demonstrated that when people practice mindfulness meditation, they produce a very high ratio of the anterior part of the Theta brainwave.[11] Therefore, practicing mindfulness every day as a menu in our lives will bring many benefits.

Practicing mindfulness can bring benefits and improve a number of mental illnesses including: Learning to let go; Creating distance from thoughts, feelings, and behaviors; Reducing judgment; Increasing awareness of bodily states; Increasing awareness and regulating emotional states; and Calm awareness of present moment. With mindfulness can improve health problems: Anxiety and chronic stress.[12]

♥ Quiet Mind

Practicing mindfulness as a marathon runner, it takes perseverance and patience in one's self. In other words, the practice of mindfulness does not try to reach a state at all, there is no need to desire to go anywhere, and there is no need to run through time to attain any wisdom or goal. We merely want to call ourselves back to the fullness of the present, when the body and mind are one. Then there is a calm mind, and mindfulness and calm happen in this moment here and now.

When you practice mindfulness diligently with a with plan, then tranquility and calmness will naturally develop in a very natural and profound way. Especially when one knows how to dwell in stillness and observe without reaction or criticism. When the mind is clear, you have the knowledge to see a problem clearly, and you will definitely make the right decisions.

The spirit of mindfulness is to practice only to practice. Bringing the mind back to the breath to naturally receive each moment in parallel with the awareness of whether the mood is going to be pleasant or unpleasant, good or bad. Identify it simply because that is what is really present in you right now. With this attitude, you are training the mind to become mature, a state of calm mind. And then, instead of you being a mindful practitioner, mindfulness will return to guide your life, or in other words, life itself becomes meaningful when mindfulness enlightens and guides you.

With a calm mind brought up by mindfulness practice, you can achieve inner peaceful states such as: Non-attachment; Quieting the mind; Minimize internal self-talk; Non-striving; Creating distance from the ego-mind; and Restful Alertness.

Healing wounds of mental health: Chronic pain; Personality disorders; Obsessive-compulsive disorder; Substance abuse; and Eating disorders.[13]

♥ Pay attention

Concentration is an ability of the mind to help us maintain our attention to an object of observation without distraction. To become centered by practicing your attention on the breath, consciously cling to the breath in and out.[14] Following the breath, the mind has room to rely on and no longer wanders in the flow of emotions. In the Sanskrit and Pāli language this is called *samadhi*, which means to focus attention on one point. This is not easy for beginners to the practice of mindfulness meditation, since our minds have long enjoyed flying and releasing outside. When you tell yourself to sit here, it is harder than running for ten miles. However, if you persevere in trying to hold on to the breath, just watch the breath going in, the breath coming out, just practice like that. In the course of practice, sometimes after only a few breaths, the mind will run away, then you quickly invite the mind back to the breath, continue to go on, your mind will stay with the breath.

Without attention (concentration), our mindfulness will not be persistent. But when there is stillness and peace brought by the attention (focus), it will be a solid foundation for mindfulness. When the mind wanders from place to place, return to the breath to restore concentration. The deeper the concentration of mind, the deeper awareness of mindfulness.

The experience of a state of deep concentration gives us a very pleasant peace. When the mind becomes calm, then all thoughts and feelings will disappear. Samadhi is often described as an integration into a state of stillness and unshakeable joy. The miracle of this tranquility of peace can be very seductive, sometimes making us fascinated. The experience of Zen teachers in the Buddhist tradition describe this state as food of bliss of mindful meditation, meaning meditation is the spiritual food that can bring nourishment and happiness. Therefore, we find ourselves interested in finding this peaceful feeling, which is very simple state of peace and joy.

Studies have shown that a person's brain waves are in a state of attention or concentration due to mindfulness meditation practice, which can create an increase in the connection between the front and the back of the brain in gamma brain waves at levels 20 to 30 hertz.

Concentration may be appropriate for those who have cognitive issues such as attention issues, working memory, or distraction. If we consider the attention deficit hyperactivity disorder (ADHD), the practice of mindfulness meditation can improve this symptom and help the patient have connections that become apparent.

As stated, the practice of concentration is to focus on an object like the breath, and when the concentration is lost, the awareness is lost, then return to focus on the breath. This practice is very helpful for people with ADHD symptoms. Psychiatrists or meditation teachers recommend that people with ADHD practice following each step slowly to bring the mind back to the body. The breathing exercise pays attention to each step. When taking one step, pay attention to the action preparing to bring the foot up, stepping up and putting the foot down. Practicing this for a while, the brain will change, the brain waves will slow down. So mindfulness is a great way to treat people with ADHD symptoms.[15]

Research shows us that concentration can have benefits such as: Develop mental stability; Improve cognitive self-awareness; Improve concentration and focus; Increase self-monitoring; Increase sustained attention; Reducce mind wandering; and Reduce distractibility.[16]

Attention can help to cope with some mental illnesses such as: Attention deficit hyperactivity disorder – ADHD; Cognitive decline in elderly; Memory problems; and Mild traumatic brain injury.[17]

♥ The opening of the heart

Kindness and compassion are gained through the practice of mindfulness meditation, which scientists measure as the opening of the heart. When the heart is open, it involves activities including tolerance, generosity and forgiveness for oneself and willingness to help others.[18] Because this practice is closely related to the attention and sharing of some concentrated brainwave patterns.

Open heart mindfulness meditations are sometimes described as a component of mindfulness practice.[19] It has been shown that brainwave activity of experienced meditators increase in gamma wave communication from the back of the brain that increases the power of brain waves gamma.[20]

There is a certainty between the two voluntary control practices of attention and cognitive processes.[21] The practice of opening the heart is different from meditation mindfulness, focusing on a systematic and conscious level of care, love and compassion. Studies have shown the difference between meditation and kindness quite clearly. Mindfulness meditation opens the heart to an unconditional sense of kindness and compassionate heart to fill the whole mind to exist, without consideration, reasoning, or other thought.[22]

Practicing mindfulness meditation opens the heart, emphasizing the establishment of a positive influence with others, which can be a great way to cure depression, sadness and other relationship problems.

The practice of open mindfulness meditation can have benefits including: Improve mood; Increase empathy; Increase generosity; Increase gratitude and appreciation; Opening the heart; and Perspective taking. Another benefit also can treat conditions like: Depression; Grief, and Personal disorders.[23]

Discussions are based on scientific research about the accuracy of the benefits of mindfulness practicing on the brain. On this basis, mindfulness is presented in detail through the lens of science, measured by state-of-the-art scientific equipment on the brains of practitioners who perennially have experienced mindfulness. The result gives us an overview of the close connection between body and mind, and we can argue that mental training by mindfulness practice has a direct effect on the brain, and the brain is the organ that determines every activity in our lives. Above all else, this practice benefits both physically and mentally. Illnesses of the mind, such as stress, anxiety, and fear, are reduced, and tolerance, calmness, and kindness are cultivated through mindfulness practice. This experience-based change corresponds to changes in brain structure and activity, which opens the door to further research into the potential of mindfulness meditation and it's benefit against the disorders people face in today's life. Hopefully this interesting study will provide information to those interested in mindfulness meditation and brain neurology.

5.

THE HEALING AWARENESS OF MINDFULNESS

Mindfulness meditation is cherished in Western countries, in part because of the benefits that science has discovered and published. But the main part of this meditation that is appealing to young people is improving their mental health. Many of us are facing serious stress because of financial difficulties, broken marriages, damaged children, overloaded work, and marketing from social networks, which have exhausted people. The miracle of this ancient meditation helps us regain balance in our lives, healing the wounds of arrows and projectiles injected into the mind. Mindfulness is a precious sword that young people can use to eliminate stress and anxiety. Because mindfulness helps us to bring our mind truly present to our body with caution and awareness in the present moment. When we are mindful, the factors that make us tired, achy, insecure, can be eliminated, that is why mindfulness as the burning of insecurities in the mind

When we practice mindfulness meditation regularly, our stress and anxiety rates will decrease, and we will increase our ability to perceive and forgive, leading to good sleep, and better relationships.[1] These benefits can help us balance our lives. Mindfulness meditation has been applied in hospitals to treat patients,[2] in school education to guide students[3] and professors,[4] and in the national social community,[5] because the practice of mindfulness is capable of cultivating concentration, being aware of everything that is happening around us, receiving life fully, making us happier and more peaceful. As good qualities are developed, we have the power to heal the wounds of the soul. Moreover, by practicing mindfulness meditation every day, we will accumulate positive energy to help us cherish life.

In everyday life when exposed to information, we are always ready to experience either the fight, flight, or freeze response. These reactions are very normal because they are available in humans, a reaction to protect our survival. Brain neuroscience shows us that sensory information is the function of the prefrontal cortex (PFC).[6] This information can help us understand neuronal functions that underlie sensory responses such as eyes, ears, nose, tongue, and then enter the thalamus sensory receptor.

The prefrontal cortex (PFC) is the cortex that covers the front of the frontal lobe. This brain area is involved in the planning of complex cognitive behavior, personality expression, decision making, empathy, compassion, and censorship of all behaviors.[7]

The thalamus function acts as a collection of sensory signals from the bottom up along with motor signals from the subcortic nucleus that cause stimulation to propagate down the spinal cord through the bundles of the medulla muscle force growth and marrow reflexes.[8]

The amygdala is a brain area mainly involved in emotional processes. It is located in the medial temporal lobe, directly in front of the hippocampus.[9]

The hippocampus consists of elongated ridges on the floor of each side ventricle of the brain, the center of emotions, memory, and the autonomic nervous system. The hippocampus, like the brain search engine, also allows for a quick and effective search among the memories stored in the new cortex, which is an essential process for future planning and brainstorming creative ideas.[10]

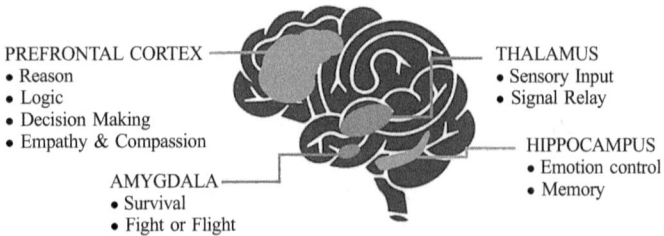

PREFRONTAL CORTEX
• Reason
• Logic
• Decision Making
• Empathy & Compassion

AMYGDALA
• Survival
• Fight or Flight

THALAMUS
• Sensory Input
• Signal Relay

HIPPOCAMPUS
• Emotion control
• Memory

Neuroscientists have shown that the impact of mindfulness meditation practice affects the brain. It should be noted that those who practice mindfulness meditation have different positive stimulation responses than those who do not practice mindfulness meditation, which have negative stimulation.

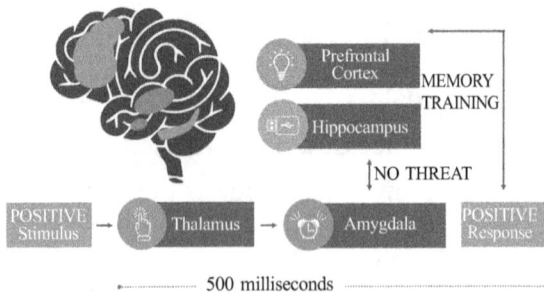

Prefrontal Cortex
MEMORY
TRAINING
Hippocampus
NO THREAT
POSITIVE Stimulus → Thalamus → Amygdala → POSITIVE Response

500 milliseconds

Response to positive stimulus

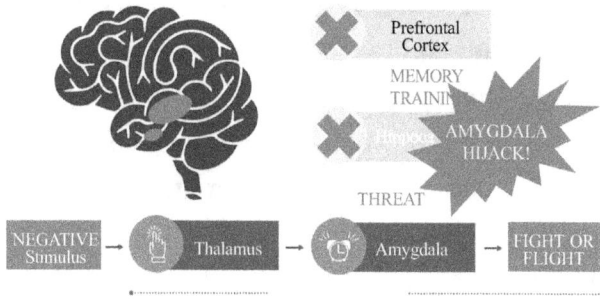

Response to negative stimulus

Mindfulness intervention helps create positive brain responses and helps practitioners deal with both positive and negative information. Dramatic or subtle, such reactions to positive stimulation and a change in perspective are indicative of full eyesight. When our mind loses interest in a negative reaction, it can be caught up in a confrontation or escape scenario. Therefore, from the miracle of mindfulness comes a change in perspective and the ability to act with greater balance and inner security, especially when faced with stress or pain or problems about mental health.

Busy lives have made us live in oblivion, the body here but the mind wandering elsewhere. Sometimes, our daily activities are like a robot, eating without knowing what food it is, looking without knowing it, because we lack mindfulness. In times of non-righteous mindfulness, if something goes wrong, the information received from the senses goes directly to the fear center and we respond by fleeing or resisting. Between stimulus and response, there is a space. In that space is our power to choose our response. In our response lies our growth and our freedom.[11] Having mindfulness, we do not react instinctively, because mindfulness is capable of helping us to care for and handle what is happening right in the moment when facing crisis.

WITHOUT MINDFULNESS

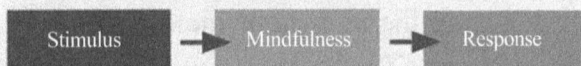

Stimulus → Response

WITH MINDFULNESS

Stimulus → Mindfulness → Response

The big difference between the way we react to unintended situations is very important, because it affects our physical and mental well-being. If we deal with anger, fear, despair, it will affect the mind, and this reaction will be stored in the store consciousness. For example, when I was young, I used to hear the cry of a neighbor woman when she was beaten by an alcoholic husband. That cry was so pitiful that it went deep into my store consciousness. Up until now, when I heard such a cry, those images came back, even though it happened decades ago. Therefore, we will feel fear, anxiety, and despair when we go through that experience again. In psychotherapy, it's called post-traumatic stress disorder (PTSD).[12] Thus, the conduct of our daily lives has a direct or indirect effect on our body and mind, or in other words, it determines our quality of life.

The healing power of mindful energy shows the benefits of mindful practice, of how to bring the transformation with a positive attitude of awareness, calmness, knowing, compassion, and perfection. Discussing mindfulness, we will outline the values of mindfulness meditation practice using the mindful breathing method (ānāpānassati). The power of this practice not only transforms your body and mind, but also directs you to a healthy, peaceful, and happy life.

♥ Bare attention

Mindfulness is an appropriate way to raise one's awareness and attention toward a better ability to experience the present moment.[13] The practitioner can instantaneously attain a simple and pure view of the object. This is a work that doesn't take much effort, but it is not easy because it is not what you usually do every day. It is a habit that you pay less attention to a true understanding of things as they are,[14] but more to the judgment of a judicial mind that benefits you. If you feel love, the mind judges it well, otherwise it can give a completely superficial and misleading look. You often put a name or brand on things that you come into contact with, which clearly shows your own mark of interest and your limited view. Most of us live with such a set of brands that shape our actions and reactions.

The merely identification attitude does not have any brand affixed to the object, it will open the door for an accurate perception. With this awareness, it will help to change yourself from a predetermined awareness to a visual awareness in one's mind when dealing with all surrounding objects. In other words, the clear mind will give you a state of mindfulness when it perceives objects with their proper function and attributes without judgment, without justification for pleasure or hatred. Simply identify the object with total attention and presence. Mindfulness is essential to that change in perception.

However, changing one's personality is not simply an instantaneous affair, but rather a regular process of mindfulness practice. Practicing the correct method will show a major change in cognitive personality when looking at the object. Practicing mindfulness meditation every morning helps your mind to calm down to start your day full of energy and insight, also helping to free you from past memories and minimizing the negative effects that come from outside. Just focus on the breathing in and out while practicing meditation, stopping all thoughts, knowing when the mind is drifting away, and bringing it back. The results of this practice will help you to expand to reflect on the awareness, feelings, and emotions in your mind. This result will transform the doubting mind.

♥ Cultivating the mind

Mindfulness is the way to train the mind and free the mind from attachment. So practicing mindfulness leads to the true greatness of an awakened person, that is the ideal type and our dream. But to reach that ideal, you need to make an effort to practice mindfulness to change your behavior and thinking in a positive way. Mindfulness helps maintain inner stability and understanding of how mind works. Without mindfulness you will not know what is happening in the body and mind; on the contrary, if you are not mindful, you are easily influenced by external objects.

Having mindfulness, you control yourself, and you are not dominated by the situation. Lacking mindfulness, one cannot control oneself, and is caught up in external circumstances. Like a branch that flows in a river, if that branch is not caught in reeds on either side of the river, then it is completely capable of drifting straight into the great sea. The mindful one, too, without being disturbed by external obstacles, will have a mind at peace.

Thus, it is this soul who needs to be trained to develop wholesome living, to adjust and cleanse by practicing mindfulness to lead a noble and virtuous life.[15] A truly happy person is a master of emotions, who has a deep understanding of the mind's awareness and a rich life experience. Through mindfulness practice you can dispel anxiety, fears, and insecurities. When your mind is not resting with your body, it is immersed in thinking about painful memories from the past. If you continue to think without being aware of that line of thought, you will be more worried and more insecure. Mindfulness energy has the ability to bring you back to the present moment. When you return to the present moment, you will be free from the endless thoughts of the mind. Suffering only comes knocking on the door when you remember the past or worry for the future, but experience right in the present moment has nothing to bother you at all. Yesterday was history, tomorrow is something very mysterious, but today is a valuable gift to live. When the mind is present in the present moment you are able to do what you want, to find courage, hope, and a right choice of life.

A very noble truth that mindfulness offers you, is to keep your mind calm in every situation so that you can become self-adaptive. No matter how talented and clever you are, you still have clumsiness and shortcomings. Moreover, life always has unintended and unsatisfactory things come knocking on the door, and you become stuck when you do not have enough energy to deal with these external factors. Without energy, you often react negatively when faced with difficulties. But if you have a lot of awakening energy, you will be calm enough to see the problem and solve the problem in the right way. This can be done by anyone. Life is inherently changing constantly. With mindfulness, we clearly see every situation that happens, whether joyful or excited or angry, and will not act in a way to hurt people. The state of emotions will always be kept in the most balanced state, the mind waves will be calmed, then you will be calmed and firmly established and in control.

Mindfulness can fully grasp the truth in life that always moves, and you are completely unaffected by any change in time, because you understand that life is originally a journey of finding love, power, happiness, respect, praise, etc., forming a closed circle with no way out. All of that comes from the need as a mind food, it's nothing new. Mindfulness is based on grasping these two factors, stopping all thoughts, and contemplating deeply, then you overcome all suffering and attain peace and happiness in life. The mind training message gives you the best understanding and awareness through:

To know the mind: That there are things that happen very closely in life, but you never know if you don't have mindfulness.

To shape the mind: It is very difficult to grasp and very stubborn, however, you can tame the mind easily through practicing mindfulness.

To free the mind: The mind is always in a state of being bound and attached to the environment; however, it is liberated from that attachment by the power of mindfulness.[16]

If you want to achieve happiness and peace in life, the basic and necessary thing is to understand how the mind works. Because the mind is the root to form everything. By understanding the mind then everything else will naturally follow. The mind is just like the roots of a tree and all the branches, leaves, flowers, and fruits depend on the roots. If you take care to nourish the roots well, the tree will sprout and produce delicious fruits. If you cut the roots, the tree will die quickly. Those who understand the behavior of the mind easily obtain happiness and peace in life. On the contrary, it is difficult for you to attain true peace and happiness once the mind is still dependent on external factors, or in other words, you are not in control of your own happiness. Because all good or evil is coming from the mind, it cannot be found anywhere but the mind. It is like the law of cause and effect; if the clear mind produces good things, the greedy mind will have dark thoughts. The unpolluted mind is one who is awakened, capable of transforming suffering to experiencing a peaceful life. People who are still entangled by polluted minds will suffer from much unhappiness in life.

♥ Transforming emotions

Brain neuroscience has shown that people who are able to manage their emotions in different situations are more likely to succeed in life, from work to family life, and connect with all walks of life. Controling emotions is an important thing to bring about happiness, and the practice of mindfulness meditation every day, rather than a high intelligence quotient (IQ), can aid in this endeavor.[17] In Buddhism, this is not surprising, because when the mind is rested in tranquility and clarity, it is aware of all true emotions, all actions such as words, volitions, thoughts are performed from consciousness without being driven by emotion. That life skill is for all of us who can do it to achieve a life of true health and wellbeing.

In our minds we contain all wholesome and unwholesome seeds. Seeds of compassion, joy, wisdom; and also the seeds of fear, anxiety, and difficulty.[18] You may be a person who is completely in control of your emotions, becoming a saint, or you may be an unhappy slave to your emotions. When a person is described as a faithful person, this does not mean that he or she has no seed of betrayal. The other person having an open mind of forgiveness does not mean that he does not have the seeds of hatred and pettiness. The problem is how you care and water the seeds.

We know that every day in the United States, about 120 people commit suicide,[19] many of them young. They end their lives by failing to control their emotions when faced with difficulties. Feelings of discomfort, anger, anxiety, pain, despair, and fear can strike a person who does not have enough energy to support him. We humans are made up of many factors such as form, feeling, perception, mind, and recognition, called form, sensation, perception, action, and consciousness. Emotions are just one of the very small mental factors in this human being. So, we need to learn how to transform those emotions. First of all, we need to realize that emotion is just a feeling that comes for a while and then it goes away. It brings awareness to be aware when it is present, as a sign that the sky is about to have snowstorms or heavy rains. When you notice these signs, you have to prepare for the storms, so you can sit back and watch your breathing in the breathing exercises in chapter 2. Practicing mindful breathing, naturally coming and going within a few breaths, the mind will calm down, recognize the emotion, and it will slowly disappear. We are no longer suffering from the storm of emotional attacks. It is the art of transforming emotions through the method of practicing mindfulness. Knowledge alone does not change our behavior and attitudes, but it is understanding of mind and mindfulness that can change or transform the storm of emotions.

♥ Awareness of anger

Anger is a psychological emotional reaction to unintended, intense emotions that go beyond the person's limit. Anger is a powerful emotion that causes inhibition, hurt, sorrow, collapse in one's own life, and the ability to hurt other people. A person who holds anger in his heart is like one holding a knife to cut his flesh, hurting himself and also hurting his opponent. Anger is like a fire burning, burning your mind, burning everything close to you. It distracts the human brain, makes all thoughts become impatient, impatient in every activity and communication

We rarely devote attention to find the true source of anger, instead, often assume that the situation itself, that another person, has made us angry. In almost every situation, we attribute all responsibility of anger to the perceived enemy. The reaction of anger is revenge, so we often find a way to respond with an action or word that makes the opponent hurt, the more painful the more satisfied. This action wants to prove you're a strong, brave person, It is also a conditional response to protect yourself from injury the next time. However, in reality, when the anger is still there, the response only makes things more and more confused and makes us exhausted and tired. When we're angry, our energy is burned out, our body releases adrenaline and cortisol, which causes a circadian cycle disorder, a sudden increase in heart rate and breathing, and stressful muscle bundles leading to tremor, shaking. We can fall into a light coma, see things untrue, think less clearly, and even worse, we are not in control of our behavior.

For some jobs, such as the police, the amount of adrenaline usually rises when they are in a state of constant vigilance, concern for the security of others and protection for themselves. Similar to police work, this also happens to people who have to do many things at the same time. They are always trained to be alert for possible bad situations but never think that good things will come. In fact, the majority of the time things are good and peaceful. Everyone has a certain amount of adrenaline in our body, but when a situation affects it, causing it to rise, it takes at least twenty-four hours to return to normal. Each day we take less than ten hours to rest and must continue to work. Increased adrenaline can help us be a bit active, work hard. But when we step out of our working environment and return to ourselves, we seem to lose all energy, become listless and depressed. In the United States before 2016, the number of police officers who committed suicide increased four times more while on duty.[20]

The breath is a safe return point whenever you are attacked by angry storms, when you do not know what to do. When you know that anger is present, instead of trying to fight back, you return to your breath, calming your mind by breathing gently, in order to reduce the heart rate, reduce the tension of the nerves, thereby reducing the negative emotions harmful to the body. Pay close attention to the process when anger is present, and carefully observe the actions, words, and thoughts we want to perform in the meantime. By cuddling the anger, like cuddling a crying child to comfort, with awareness, it will slowly calm down. With mindful energy you will discover that anger is just a source of energy generated by a few misconceptions or an exaggerated imagination, where we are unable to control emotions and sensory senses outside to find satisfaction. Therefore, simply maintaining the mindfulness ability to observe the process of anger with an unbiased attitude, you will see the roots of anger and easily transform them.

♥ Relieve the pain with a compassionate heart

Every one of us has experienced suffering. Sometimes the pain does not just stop at the body but also torments the soul, making your life unbalanced. By practicing mindfulness, you can recognize your own pain, then cultivate compassion to ease that pain. Here compassion represents love, charity, kindness, tolerance, and such noble qualities on the emotional side.[21]

Practicing mindfulness increases compassion and alleviates suffering, especially the emotions that cause insecurity and suffering. With mindfulness and concentration, we can tolerate the weaknesses of our self, and neutralize resentment and hatred from others. Thus, mindfulness not only helps us to see the root of pain, it also increases our tolerance for ourselves and others. When the mind is calm, you will see that compassion not only nourishes the warmth in the mind, the thoughts, but also the action. Wherever we are, we need love to warm the pain and insecurity in our spiritual life. Everyone knows that compassion can only be nourished by letting go of a small selfish mind and sharing, caring for others. Your joy is also my joy, your pain is also my pain. Therefore, one who can love oneself is capable of loving others, and then this world will draw us closer together and will be filled with peaceful sunshine.

♥ Overcoming selfishness

Selfishness is one of the illnesses that makes our mind small, rarely sharing material, knowledge, and understanding to others. Because we do not yet see the nature of dependent origination, we cling to things that we think are our own, and then create conceit and selfishness. When you look at a corn plant, you think that the corn plant is made up of its own essence. But when you look more closely, you can see that the corn exists because of many other factors, including fertilizer, minerals, air, the effort of the farmer, caring, watering, and even the nutrients from decaying waste. Thanks to external factors, the corn is nourished, developed, and survived. Without one of these factors, the corn would not exist. Although corn is grown from corn kernels, corn plants and their ancestors are also based on countless other conditions from the sky to mature. Corn has never existed alone. The truth is that there is no independent existence at all, everything depends on each other. Corn is also made up of conditions other than corn.

If the corn plant knows the fact that it is the external factors that provide the nutrients it needs to support its growth, it also recognizes that it is a union of roots, stems, and branches, and many other things, and it will never flap its chest proudly, arrogantly, and live selfishly. Because without one of the external conditions, the corn plant may die at any time. The corn plant represents only one physiognomy that represents all that the ancestors of the corn plants and the earth gave. When understanding that the general appearance only manifests for a while and then changes to another status, the corn plants always live their best, loving roots, leaves, branches, stems and everything else around them. The corn tolerates heavy rains, intense sunlight, or hurricanes so that it can grow strong and produce delicious, sweet corn. Corn plants live very proud, acutely aware of their environment, and devote themselves to life.

Have you ever wondered where is your talent comes from? Do you train hard, or do you learn from teachers and friends while sitting on the school chair, or receive the seeds of talent from ancestors passed down through the generations? When you can write calligraphy or cook a pot of noodles, you must know that the ancestors also wrote calligraphy and used to cook rice noodles. The scientists say that you have nearly seventy percent of the fusion cells that are similar to your parents, and that your lifestyle and cognition are the same. But sometimes you get angry, saying that he is not my father, or not my son. It is a selfishness.

Like corn, we are also a continuation from ancestors and need many other external factors to exist rather than a separate entity. The only difference is that we inherit the seeds of the previous generation plus new elements such as the educational environment, culture, training to create a new life, a new mission. In other words, in order to carry out a mission of our life, our friend's life will constantly meet and be affected by the laws of the universe. To become a socially appropriate person and to devote talents to the country, we must rely on other fields such as economy, education, society, politics, and religion.

❤ Letting go

The information that occurs in everyday life is brought to the mind, and then the data plays back exactly like a television channel from one program to another. The senses are capable of storing events in a discreet way, beautiful memories of childhood or great pictures of a trip. At the same time, your memory also records those who have hurt you, those harmed by you, or your desolate mood. In other words, it is full of fragrant flowers and also contains trash. It is a strange thing that people tend to remember bad things, like rubbish, rather than enjoy the fragrance of beautiful flowers. Bad events are more attractive and influential than exciting events are. Negative thoughts quickly become habits and they are more difficult to change than the positive.

Negative emotions keep us immersed in anxiety, doubt, fear, and despair. When we return to sad memories, we tend to seek clarity, seek reasoning, analyze them over and over, then deduce the consequences in a completely opposite way, not reflecting on the nature of the possible problem. We feel like experiencing that pain once more again, that sad sign emerges, our breath becomes chaotic, our body is cold, our intestines are tightened, and the internal television screen looks exactly like what happened the first time. It does not stop there, for at night we still have nightmares, and your life becomes shaken because of not sleeping well.

Now, think of a wonderful, memorable event we experienced, like watching the sun rise over the mountain on a summer morning; or the happiness on the graduation day when you receive your college degree; or remember the first anniversary of meeting your lover. Sit comfortably, breathe in and out deeply, follow the breaths in and out three times and recall any beautiful memories, the more detail you remember the more interesting you will feel. Enjoy this wonderful moment with a smile on our face. Do you feel a miracle happened? Beautiful memories make us happy; it is joyfulness in the heart which is very hard to describe! That is the joy that comes when we connect with the wonderful memories inside.

It is obvious to say that if we have mindfulness to open the door of beautiful memories every day, our life will be more joyful and happier. The challenge here is that we lack mindfulness. Instead of waking up the good things, our mind awakens the suffering of the past, the hurts, the frustrations of the past, resulting in this garbage over the other garbage. All of them become the heap of garbage which dominates and controls our life.

Human memory is a process of gathering memories that have been experienced over the most recent time, it is not a commentator or historian as we often think. Thinking about an event in the past gives us the feeling as watching an ongoing movie which triggers a story that happened in the past. Emotions are one of the most complex matters of the brain that cause people a lot of troubles. Memory is not a recorder that can record everything we experience in our daily life, but memory is just an editorial inspiration that filters and stores the data that comes every day in its own way. Whenever we think about those things it rewrites a completely different story from the initial one. Therefore, remembering an event that happened in the past, we rarely recollect that memory intact as it was, but we are recalling our latest memory of that. So, the masters often say that every time repeated it is totally new story.

Remember, we memorize events in an improper and inaccurate way than how the events occurred. The senses are capable of storing memories of good and evil, and the function of knowingly preserving them is very carefully done. The challenge is how in everyday life can you touch good memories? Since the human brain has a very sensitive alert system, it often emits problems that are not true to the physical as well as the psychological. The sensibility of the brain makes it easy for people to associate misconceptions and misleading conclusions, which are the causes of suffering. If you do not have mindfulness practice to clearly see the functioning of the brain, grieving events can still leave your mind writhing for a long time, even if the causes of that worry have calmed down.

Mindfulness has the potential to help us to understand that the brain is constantly receiving and sending subconscious cues in your everyday gestures, actions, thoughts. Mindfulness helps you to understand that your initial emotional response to those warning signals can be unconscious, as your brain connects your memories with a self-defense tendency. Every day, the brain habitually and automatically emits thousands of images and thoughts. Emotions, images that catch your attention, or things that you try to suppress or deny. When you understand the functioning of the brain, it is possible to let go of negative memories. Then we do not have to be upset to analyze, to face the constant problems in our daily life.

Thus, mindfulness is the door to our happiness, the key to free you from *junk trucks* in the past. We do not need to run away from bad memories or suppress negative thoughts whenever they appear, but rather just smile, wave, and walk toward the way we are aiming. When we have the ability to let go of sad memories, we will have confidence and happiness in life. Many of us tend to be too serious about problems, always concentrating on the current difficulties and self-drawing an insecure future for ourselves

To improve negative thoughts in our life, you need to identify the difficult issues that you are facing. When you are aware of the cause, we can find a solution to the problem. Remember that we cannot avoid the things that make us depressed, anxious, and frustrated, because that is part of life. With the awareness, we will not allow these negative thoughts effect our energy any time, and our life will be happier and more peaceful.

6.

THE ROLE OF MINDFULNESS IN EDUCATION

Mindfulness-based programs in schools are a growing field, which is evident by the rapid increase of mindfulness in the field of education around the world. This increased interest in mindfulness is due to the apparent benefits being uncovered through the growing number of reports, publications, and articles on the subject. Until recently, the study of mindfulness and its effects on an educational environment was inconsistent, as programs were not implemented in the whole school, and were not continued as an integral part of the school's curriculum and culture.[1] It may be that a whole school mindfulness-based model in education is a relatively new concept, but this is the best framework for students and faculty that has been defined, applied, and studied. When designed by the principle, a full integration of mindfulness in the school curriculum, including engagement of school teachers, incorporation of parents, and a gradual long-term process which influences the school's culture and climate, it is possible to have sustained success in improving student quality of life.[2] This paper describes how mindfulness-based programs have been improved to help students who have faced mental health problems and reduce teacher burnout. This technique is extremely important and can become an integral part of a school's curriculum if the organization wants to promote a positive mental health setting in education. The following questions guided my inquiry: Which students face mental health challenges that affect their studies in an educational environment? And how have mindfulness-based programs been improved to help students who face mental health challenges?

To find answers to these questions, I will review the documents and related literature using the following search key words: mindfulness in education, curriculum, implementation, and grounded theory. My plans are to do qualitative interviews to capture the experiences of student's practicing mindfulness to hear how this technique improves their mental health problems.

♥ Students face challenges with mental health problems

Many students are already suffering because our society values doing over being, and product over process. As researchers argue, our culture tends to put test scores, wealth, and status before joy, connection, and well-being. Scientific research and the media tell us that young people's lives are increasingly stressful.[3] For some, stress and depression are simply outcomes of living in our fast-paced, media-saturated society. For others, the stress comes from being pushed to perform and succeed in getting into a great school. Unfortunately, this stress also involves surviving in extremely challenging, even traumatic, home environments and life circumstances. Other research indicates that regardless of race, education, or socioeconomic status, an alarming number of adolescents are being diagnosed with attention deficit hyperactivity disorder (ADHD), stress, depression, anxiety, obesity, eating disorders, addictions, and other self-destructive behaviors, including suicidal tendencies.[4]

International students are particularly at risk, as they face challenges with cultural adjustment, social isolation, and academic difficulties. The first year of college in particular presents many challenges, such as language barriers when communicating with professors and loneliness in class due to difficulties engaging in conversation with fellow students. International students deal with differences in approaches to studying, such as when they engage in group assignments. They face obstacles as they pursue higher education outside of their home countries such as different food, unfamiliar living circumstances, financial problems, balancing work, studying schedules, learning styles, or any difficulties related to culture and personal barriers.[5] In addition, foreign students also "suffered from emotional and physical stress which resulted in tiredness, lack of sleep, role conflict, homesickness and frustration."[6]

It is clear that the U.S. educational system is currently facing many challenges related to student mental health. Here in the U.S., college students seeking mental health services report that anxiety is their primary concern and it is on the rise. Researchers who surveyed almost 14,000 first-year college students found that 35 percent struggled with a mental illness, particularly depression or anxiety. College students seeking mental health services report that anxiety is their #1 concern and it is on the rise. [7]

According to data from the U.S Department of Education Office of Civil Rights, between 2011 and 2012, 3.45 million students received out-of-school suspension and 3.5 million received in-school suspension. [8] This stress impedes learning and undermines physical and mental health, including:

"25% of teenagers suffer from anxiety disorders; 6.5 million children struggle from disabilities that impair their ability to learn; One in four high school students has been offered, sold or given illegal drugs on school property; One in three children are either overweight or obese; Nearly 3 million students receive medication for attention deficit hyperactivity disorder (ADHD); Suicide is the third leading cause of death among teenagers; High-stress levels also damage teachers and educators, resulting in extremely high burnout rates." [9]

Even with the mindfulness technique offering a potential solution for improving student mental health, there are issues to implementing a mindfulness system. With demands for mental health support typically exceeding resources, what can we do to bring mindfulness techniques that address student well-being both inside and outside of our schools? What are the best strategies, practices, and resources to implement a mindfulness-based program in the field of education?

Research suggests there is a need for programs to help students respond calmly to unsettling and provocative student behavior and not inadvertently escalate these behaviors by their reactions.[10] This is where mindfulness can be most effective.

♥ Why we should be practicing mindfulness?

One's success is also partially influenced by racial genetics, the educational environment where he grew up, and the status of his family. A successful person also has good influence when he has good academic achievement and high intelligence quotient. As Thomas Edison once said, "Genius is one percent inspiration, ninety-nine percent perspiration." But the most important factor of a successful person is passion, self-made, working hard, persistence, and stable love relationships in both mental and physical health. These people can focus on work enthusiastically, pay attention and control their emotions consciously very well.

Mindfulness meditation helps us focus and relate to life. It is easy to understand if you are treated to a big meal or professor Dr. Richard Davidson lectures on meditation related to brain nerves. If you do not pay attention and focus, then how can you enjoy the delicious food, how you can understand the lecture of the professor?

Mindfulness meditation exercises aim to train your brain to focus, pay attention, and control your emotions, which is the foundation for learning, and for all success in life. Thus, mindfulness meditation helps you to be awake to enjoy life and to succeed in life. So why don't we practice mindfulness meditation?

Mindfulness meditation comes from Eastern cultural traditions. Mindfulness is the chief factor in the practice of satipatthana,[11] the best-known system of Buddhist meditation, as taught by the Buddha who lived and taught in northeast India in the fifth century BC.[12] Mindfulness meditation first appeared as a therapeutic subject in 1979, when Dr. Jon Kabat-Zinn introduced it as Mindfulness– Based Stress Reduction at the University of Massachusetts Medical Center.[3] Today, mindfulness meditation is studied and taught all around the world. Famous universities such as Harvard, Stanford, Massachusetts Institute of Technology (MIT), Yale, Oxford, Cambridge, and many other universities have applied this practical mindfulness meditation method to professors, lecturers, students, and interns.

The University of Oxford, United Kingdom, has the Center of Mindfulness Oxford,[13] where a master's degree on mindfulness is offered. This program is not about religious research; it is not about the uselessness or accidentally that the professors devote themselves to the study of Mindfulness meditation if there are no practical benefits. The lens of science has shown us that mindfulness practice reduces depression, anxiety, and stress; increases feelings of happiness, joyfulness, concentration, focus, and an ability to achieve well in school.[14] The mindfulness course at Oxford teaches friendly attention skills to what happens in the mind, body, and surroundings. Awareness of the present moment helps us to understand how the mind works, skillfully responding to stress and difficulties, and mindfulness allows us to enjoy happiness, contentment, gratitude, and balance in facing of the ups and downs of life.[15]

The development of modern technology has negatively affected personal life with a focus on the things outside that distract the mind. Things that are considered modern like Smartphones, iPads, Laptops, and social media networks like Facebook, Instagram, Twitter, are now a major focus for our youth, who seem to be constantly tapped into them. The whispering voices inside our mind never stop working; the ability to focus and pay attention on a subject is not easy at all, and it requires skill and practice every day.

Therefore, the ability of students to listen to the teachers' lectures in class, concentrate on writing articles, or remembering formulas, are even more difficult. It requires constant training. Mindfulness can help us do this. When the mind is distracted, simply return to the normal breath, then realize it, then immediately return to reality. Many people say that I do not need to practice mindfulness because it is already inside me.

Indeed, humans generally have an extraordinary intelligence and are highly adaptable. The nirvana of Buddha nature is already in the human store consciousness.[16] However, people rarely use all their inherent abilities. We know that Stephen Hawking, a genius of the 21st century, continued working every day. Cristiano Ronaldo is a great football player, but he still practices consistently every day. Mindfulness is not only the ability to concentrate and pay attention, but also the ability to feel emotions such as pain, anger, frustration, anxiety, fear, but not react foolheartedly to them.

School programs only focus on teaching students the specialized subjects of reading, writing, math, and research, which mostly neglect the necessary matters such as attention, self-control of emotion, consciousness, positive thought, and knowledge about brain activities.[17]

Mindfulness meditation helps us manage our emotions and respond appropriately when facing anything, which helps calm us down before speaking or acting. In life we are often dominated by emotions, but we forget that emotions are constantly changing. Sadness and joy come and go like ocean waves. Mindfulness meditation helps us to see its true nature, or in other words, mindfulness meditation allows you to walk on the waves, not submerge yourself in the ocean.

♥ Outcome of the mindfulness technique in education

Mindfulness meditation means knowing your conception of life, being aware of the fullness of every moment in life, being in touch with reality and what is happening around you.[18] Practicing mindfulness continuously in daily life will create a strong capacity to awaken inside and connect with objects happening around you in a clear sense. The awareness gained by practicing mindfulness is described as open-hearted.[19] Awakening not only adds attention to oneself, but it also aids in the non-judgmental acceptance and forgiveness of the external and even the inner self. The important thing is that strong compassion is shown by caring for the people around us. Studies of mindfulness meditation show the practical benefits in psychological health,[20] stress management,[21] attentional abilities, and maintaining emotional balance.[22]

Over the years, the need of teaching attention and management of emotions has been taken into consideration. Many mindfulness programs have been developed and applied specifically for teachers and students. The purpose of these programs is to provide teachers and students with a lesson plan called the habits of mind,[23] to support emotional balance, and create a healthy environment for learning and teaching effectively. The highlight is training teachers to be comfortable and motivated in teaching. This is obvious, because teachers are an important foundation for any educational institution, because it is the teacher who plays a guiding role for students who are motivated to develop their academic aptitude.[24] Many mindfulness-based educational initiatives that start off with a team of teachers, like mindfulness for teachers,[25] have proven successful in influencing teachers. Mindfulness meditation has reduced stress and increased the ability to care for students,[26] and manage students with more quality.[27] Once the teachers have a calm mind to understand what students need in the classroom, they not only provide knowledge, but also develop creativity, ethical personality, and learn how to handle their emotions properly. When teachers play that role, they are able to teach students the basics of attention, the ways to regulate emotions, and to create harmonious relationships in the classroom.[28]

The practicing of mindfulness meditation helps students succeed in their studies,[29] such as being more attentive in lessons, being able to control stress and negative emotions.[30] A peaceful atmosphere is created in the classroom when students and teachers practice mindfulness together.

Many mindfulness programs apply to students such as *The Quiet Time Changes Lives.*[31] The purpose of this program is to improve academic performance and reduce stress and violence[32] in the field of education. This is a training program for teachers to practice mindfulness meditation using the breath mindfulness method and then apply it to students.

Stress is a contributing factor to mental and physical illness, and it is also the number one enemy that impedes learning. It destroys and ruins the bright future of so many children. In developed cities, due to the school's need for high standards, the professionalism of teaching requires higher professionalism compared to three decades ago. The number of students who do not prepare homework for school increases the many serious personality problems. Research shows that many teachers are faced with difficulty in mastering their emotions in the classroom when students are not paying attention to the lecture. This situation creates a stifling atmosphere, the ability to teach and learn decreases and making teachers feel burnout cascade.[33] Where urban schools are low-income, traumatic stress is a reality for millions of children who grow up in poverty, violence and fear.[34] This stress hinders learning and undermines the physical and mental well-being of students.

The results of mindfulness techniques show us the practical benefits that have been demonstrated by applying meditation to students and teachers, reporting surprising results.

- *10% improvement in test scores and GPA*
- *Increased attendance and decreased suspensions for high school students*
- *Reduced ADHD symptoms and symptoms of other learning disorders*

- *Increased intelligence and creativity*
- *40% reduction in psychological distress, including stress, anxiety and depression*
- *Reduction in teacher burnout and perceived stress.*[35]

The application of meditation in the field of education not only shows results improving in stress, anxiety, and depression, but also shows that creativity develops, even memory attention is increased, and this confidence contributes to classwork. Professor James S. Dierke, Executive Vice President of the United States School Administration Association, said that: *"The Quiet Time program is the most powerful, effective program I've come across in my 40 years as a public-school educator. It is nourishing these children and providing them an immensely valuable tool for life. It is saving lives."*[36]

Given the scale of this mental health crisis, there is real urgency to innovate new approaches where there is good preliminary evidence. Mindfulness fits this criterion and we believe there is enough evidence of its potential benefits to warrant a significant scaling-up of its availability in schools.[37]

Many private and public-school organizations have introduced mindfulness meditation to students and teachers under different names all for the same purpose of improving academic and teaching achievement in today's educational environment in the United States and around the world. Here are ten reasons why mindfulness meditation should be applied to schools:

- *reduce stress in the classroom.*
- *improve student's concentration.*
- *enhance focus.*
- *strengthen memory.*
- *develop harmony & improve relationships.*
- *introduce a lifelong method to reduce stress.*
- *create a quiet time during the day.*
- *recharge the student's mind.*
- *offer staff the time to experience relaxation.*
- *lower anxiety around exam time.*[38]

The Dalai Lama once said that if every 8-year-old in the world is taught meditation, we will eliminate violence from the world within one generation.[39] The role of mindfulness meditation is very important in the school environment, as it is the nutrition of the lives for students and teachers. Practicing mindfulness meditation is an art to remove stress, help us relax and refresh. When stress is calmed, teachers become interested and love to pass on instruction to students, and students are also motivated to learn instead of fleeing.

A test of a group of 137 students practicing mindfulness meditation aged 17-19 in the United States showed fatigue and negative emotions such as sadness, fear, anxiety, guilt, and disgust, anxiety and anger were reduced, and calmness, relaxation, acceptance and emotional regulation were increased.[40] In other studies, just practicing mindfulness meditation twice a day for 15 to 30 minutes, can reduce stress and aid in being more creative, calm, relaxed and motivated in activities.[41] Thus, mindfulness meditation helps you grasp the key to a better health both mentally and physically.

♥ Implementation

The United States and the United Kingdom are among the countries that have led the innovation in introducing mindfulness meditation into schools with a variety of programs everywhere from preschool, elementary, high school, to university. The extensive mindfulness curriculum ranges from the instructor's brief mindfulness meditation practice with a class, to being broadcast on the radio before the classes start.

There are many mindfulness programs you can refer to for instructors, students, and administrators, or for your own training. There are some online, some use audio recordings, and some require classroom training directly.

Summary of the mindfulness-based programs:

Name	Applying for	The brief outcomes of a program
1. Association for mindfulness in Education[42]	K-12	This program is a collaborative association of organizations and individuals working together to provide support for mindfulness training as a component of K-12 education.
2. Calmer Choice[43]	Teachers and students	Cultivating awareness, living mindfully, and enhancing resilience
3. Care for Teachers[44]	Teachers	Cultivating Awareness and Resilience in Education – (CARE) is a unique professional development program that helps teachers handle the stresses and rediscover the joys of teaching.

4. Compassionate schools project[45]	elementary and secondary students	is the most comprehensive study ever undertaken of a 21st-century health and wellness curriculum in an elementary or secondary school setting.
5. Cultivating Awareness and Resilience in Education[46]	Teachers	mindfulness-based professional development program to help teachers deal with stress and stimulate joy in teaching.
6. Inner explorer[47]	PreK-12	practice skills such as self-care and appropriate handling of negative emotions such as stress, anxiety, anger, frustration, sadness, and more.
7. Inner Kids[48]	Kids and Family	pragmatic approach to sharing mindfulness with the whole family
8. Inner Resilience[49]	Students and teachers	cultivate the inner lives of students, teachers, and schools by integrating Social and Emotional Learning (SEL) with contemplative practice.
9. Inward Bound Mindfulness Education[50]	Teens and adults	Learn awareness, compassion, and concentration practices on a residential retreat

10. Leaning to Breathe[51]	Adolescents	is a research-based mindfulness curriculum created for classroom or group setting.
11. Mindful Life Project[52]	Children	Empower underserved children through mindfulness and other transformative skills to gain self-awareness, confidence, self-regulation, and resilience, leading to lifelong success.
12. Mind with Heart Mind[53]	Students and Teachers	A place to train teachers and students about sustainable welfare, emotional health, and social community connection
13. Mindful Schools[54]	Children and teachers	encourage greater awareness, focused attention, and compassionate action.
14. Mindfulness-based Kindness Curriculum[55]	Students and teachers	a twelve-week course designed to train teachers and then have a certificate to teach mindfulness to students.
15. Mindfulness Everyday[56]	Children and youth	committed to improving the health and well-being of community members and the networks that support children and youth, by providing tailored mindfulness programs for students, parents, educators, and helping professionals in educational and community settings.

16. Mindfulness in Schools Project[57]	Students and teachers	learn how to bring mindfulness into your school day
17. MindUP[58]	Children and Teachers	MindUP teaches the skills and knowledge children need to regulate their stress and emotion, form positive relationships, and act with kindness and compassion.
18. Peace in Schools[59]	Teens and Adults	Transformative mindfulness education.
19. Still Quiet Place[60]	Children, teens, and adults	are kinder to themselves, and calmer and more creative when they are having difficulties with friends, family, school, sports, and other activities.
20. Stressed Teens[61]	Teens and Parents	seeking to gain greater control over their emotions and perceptions.
21. Youth Mindfulness[62]	children and adolescents	The program of training young people who are cognitive, kind, resilient, and courageous, through mindful practice, these powers can be awakened and cultivated.

22. Wake Up Schools[63]	Individuals, educators, and society	Practicing mindfulness in education is a program to support educators to bring mindfulness into school and apply morality to life to make teachers and students happier and more free.

There is a lot of experimentation and debate in the United States and the United Kingdom around the dissemination of policies, teaching methods, and practicing mindfulness meditation to suit students of many ages, primarily in university. A recent study estimates that about 2,000 people have been trained to teach mindfulness programs for young people in the UK under the auspices of government training institutions.[64]

A student shares the practical benefits of practicing mindfulness. Anaya Ali started mindfulness practice at the age of 12, and she thought it would not be as beneficial as previously said. But mindfulness practice lessons helped stabilize Anaya's mind and make her feel better. Once mindfulness became helpful, Anaya got used to it and practiced more often at home. The main reason is that mindfulness meant a great deal to her, and now, sometimes when she is stressed or over thinking, Anaya will go to her room, sit down in peace, relax her body and practice following her teacher's instructions: Focus on your breath and be aware of what is happening now. Anaya practices for about ten minutes, and when she opens her eyes, all her stress seems to overcome itself.[65]

♥ The role of mindfulness in 21st century schools

The studies on mindfulness-based stress relief programs for teachers and students have positive results and are applied by many educational institutions. It is a wonderful thing, but what we need to understand is how do teachers apply the role of mindfulness meditation in and outside of the classroom. Mindfulness should be applied in administrator offices, health care facilities, and referrals to parents to enhance the role of sustainable support for students in high schools as well as in universities.

As mentioned above, mindfulness meditation practice is related to mindfulness and the ability to create a more harmonious atmosphere both in the classroom and outside the campus. An important element of this resolute condition is kindness and compassion. When you have kindness, it is the process of awareness of difficulties and the desire to transform them. Coming home to ourselves is a very important beginning step.[66] Our habit of not being able to look at ourselves to identify difficulties, of often running away or covering up our sufferings leads to more loneliness, fear, anger and serious despair. For a teacher or a lecturer, the first thing to do is to turn back inside. The way out is in.

The practice involves turning back in order to look after yourself, learning how to create joy, happiness, peace, and learning how to heal painful wounds and emotions, listening to the pain of suffering with an understanding of a compassionate heart in order to find out where its cause comes from. Then the suffering will disappear, which is indispensable work.[67] When a teacher finds a heart wounded and has the ability to treat that wound, he will be able to understand and help the students who are facing difficulties. When a teacher confronts a crying student, with a sorrowful face, not focusing on schoolwork, showing symptoms of challenge, anger, and alienation, and not talking, reacting in a hot-tempered, frustrated manner will only make the situation worse. Mindfulness allows us to reflect deeply and not react immediately. When the mind is calm, we will find an effective solution. Calm is not alienating the emotions or not feeling them, but mindfulness allows us not to be overwhelmed by the conflicting emotions. Mindfulness is not about controlling our thoughts and emotions, but of not allowing the flow of emotions control us.

The struggle to cope with emotions is a tough process, especially for teenagers, because part of their brain used to control emotions is actually not fully developed. But somehow, feeling emotions is very mature. Therefore, when a problem happens to them, even small, it can easily turn into a big problem.[68]

With a compassionate warm heart, a teacher can be aware that training with mindfulness meditation can help students become aware of the symptoms of suffering, instead of automatically condemning them as bad behavior. The next step is to open the heart to empathize and not react to anything, try to keep the attitude fresh and create an open atmosphere. If we are not skillful in responding when confronted with a student who is struggling, we cannot empathize and cannot understand how the student's mood is; how it can be helped. So, the first very important step is to cultivate compassion.[69]

However, compassion is not enough. The next step is to regulate the emotions and to associate and sympathize with their pain. If you don't sympathize but react only superficially with pain, then how can you help others? Therefore, you need to stop to gain some calmness and observe how miserable they are in order to find ways to help. The most important thing is the task of helping students who need attention. It is putting all of them here right now to empathize with the pain of the students and listen with understanding hearts. We can solve the difficulties of others and eliminate the suffering of others, only when we have warmth and compassion and are able to listen with a wide, open heart and embrace the sufferings of other people. It is a huge difficulty to heal the school and face the student's difficulties.[70] In this way, mindfulness meditation can help us to establish compassion and provide students a wonderful compassion tool.

Compassion and kindness are not merely an interpersonal process, but they involve extending to others, the social community, and to all humanity. Kindness is the basis for awareness of community. When the heart is truly open, we are able to recognize that we are all human, equal in gender, and race, ethnicity, color, and religion. Compassion has a deeper meaning, encompassing how we care for the animals, plants, and the planet; not only focusing on how we live right now, but also caring about the future generation. Most importantly, in the field of education, compassion is a power of catalyst for teachers and students to create a healthy environment that includes equality, friendliness, and harmony in learning and teaching.

♥ The way of mindful education

We have seen over the past decades that education has failed to make an effort that can serve students well in mental health, the condition that lasts like a pandemic in an educational environment.[71] We are calling for a comprehensive transformation in the education system to bring good results. Of course, the education system needs to have change in many factors, not just relying on mindfulness meditation, kindness, and compassion. We feel that mindfulness meditation and compassion can positively contribute to the vision and framework that can change the education system in a positive way.

Mindfulness helps us see the problem more clearly, understand ourselves, and even the surrounding problems. Mindfulness also helps us have an authentic overview of the inside and outside of the campus, involving students, parents, and the entire social community. Having a clear view of relationships is a good opportunity for us to confirm what we need and to take measures to respond to challenges effectively, accurately, and promptly. Compassion provides a scene of change based on a fair sense of humanity. Mindfulness allows us to stop and think more critically when encountering difficulties and choose the path we want to take for solving the problem.

We know that students in the U.S. come from a variety of backgrounds, cultures, races, territories, languages, and customs. Many of them are surrounded by obsession with poverty, racism, and infectious diseases. Such obsession will affect the brain, and without mindfulness practice, these children cannot heal those wounds and will fall behind in their education.

I strongly believe that mindfulness can help students soothe phobia and can help them advance further. A high school student was less fortunate when his parents went to jail for drug trafficking. He was always taunted by his classmates and gave up on study because of inferiority complex. He felt frustrated, often wandering the streets alone, left out in class, and even wanting to drop out of school. But once he was introduced and instructed in the practice of mindfulness meditation, the strange thing that happened was that he returned to regular school attendance, no longer exhibiting bad behaviors in the classroom, and could be accepted in a prestigious university. The practice of mindfulness is the way to teach students to cope with their emotions, and to take away the hauntings in their heads. Their lives completely change because of awareness and learning becomes successful.

One of the problems leading to dropouts is an obsession with the unliberated mind. For some students, emotions become so overwhelming that they feel their life is permanently bad. When emotions cannot be controlled, it is easy for a student to drop out of school, and with an insufficient education the risk of living in poverty increases many times.

Educators are aware of the mental health crisis and are providing some methods that support students and leaders of schools struggling with this issue. Mindfulness is one of the effective solutions. The long-term mindfulness program has been designed from a school-wide perspective, which is a relatively new concept. It has the most effective interventions that work within the framework of health care to research and identify benefits to help students with mental health. The mindfulness-based program approach, when established in accordance with these principles, including the full integration of mindfulness in the school's curriculum, teacher involvement, and parent engagement, it is a long process that affects the culture and atmosphere in the educational environment.[72]

What is my personal experience, after asking students and teachers, what they think about mindfulness? They all share a positive feeling, they plan to continue practicing and introducing mindfulness to their loved ones, and they encourage other students to do so. The lessons are designed to help you become a mindful person, able to concentrate and pay attention, and master the emotions, rather than respond or react in a negative way, or run away.

With mindfulness, we have the ability to speak in harmony and listen deeply, which is the foundation for creating a healthy learning atmosphere and the key to establishing warm relationships in life. Eating mindfully to enjoy the taste of food is what determines your health from body to mind. When we know what we need to put in our body, then our body is healthy, the mind is clear. The breath nourishes us to be mindful in the present moment, and allows us to find peace, concentration, and control when the bad thought arises, and we know how to stop in the chaotic moments of life.

The practice of mindfulness has even more profound meaning that causes compassion to be taught, kindness to be generated, resulting in a generous altruistic heart. Therefore, we need to encourage mindfulness meditation to be taught in every school, in every city, in every state, and in every country around the world. There is no doubt about the important role of mindfulness meditation.

Each individual needs to practice mindfulness, so that we can contribute together to heal the injuries in the existing educational system. For that to happen, each individual mind must be changed and be committed. This will affect the community and change the whole world. If you have firm beliefs, like many others, the path to great success, the path to healing the mental health crisis in education, the path to a beautiful harmonious world can be found by practicing mindfulness.

The future is in your own hands. The change will happen not by chance but by your decision. Start now and start with you.

7.

MINDFUL LEADERSHIP

The concept of leadership is understood according to each person's perception. Someone can be a talented leader, creating a splendid career, but failing in his marriage. Some people are considered brilliant but may be dictators in the eyes of others. Leadership ability in private life or in a public one, can make a very positive difference to life.

Modern society witnesses changes at a dizzying pace, and there are countless challenges with the development of information technology, financial instability, and many other difficulties that make the responsibility of the leader even more important and respected. The role of a leader is to reassure people and outline better ways to solve problems that people or an organization are facing. However, it is not easy to become a successful leader. People are more skeptical of the leadership ability of senior officials in the government than in all other areas according to researchers' judgment. This is understandable because the leader is a public person, so the public always put faith in the leader, and the habitual thought is that the leader must be a good person. If that standard is not met, people reprimand or condemn.

To become a good leader, we must practice perseverance, passion for learning, and courage to learn. Thanks to that, we can resolve the disagreements smoothly, promoting the work forward. It also requires us to take responsibility, take ownership of ourselves, be strict with ourselves, and not just depend on public assessments and public opinion.

There are many people who think that it is impossible to become a leader, but we believe that anyone can become a great leader if they have the will and determination. The experience of leaders proves to us that within each temple there is a seed of nobility, which in Buddhism is called Buddha nature. That is the quality of enlightenment hidden in the mind, and it is a true, very pure nature in all of us. That person who has tapped into their true enlightened nature has the ability to understand the profound truth in the spiritual world, and is in touch with it, and thus finds the strength to continue on the path of happiness and success.

To become a leader, you need to focus on the critical and essential skillful development aspect and overcome the barriers of anxiety and fear. Psychologists say that most of us are afraid to say no to what we do not want because we are afraid to express our own negative emotions, afraid to listen to criticism of being considered silly or awkward. Certainly, all of us have experienced this fearful experience. Worry and fear are obstacles that hinder our every move. So many people think that working under someone else is less worrisome and more comfortable than being a leader. However, if we overcome your weakness and shyness, we will become strong and have the opportunity to become a leader. The best way to overcome this fear is to acknowledge that weakness is present in us, but instead of paying attention to it, focus on a leadership job that is appropriate and meaningful to us.

The power of a leader can inspire and promote the dignity of others. Great leaders often make a positive difference in an organization or community. They always appreciate the ability of others, enabling people with the capacity to work together to create common success.

William Arthur Ward[1] said: "The mediocre teacher tells. The good teacher explains. The superior teacher demonstrates. The great teacher inspires." The same is true for leaders. A leader who wants to function effectively needs to have such essential qualities as:

- Know how to focus on solving problems.

- Take care of important things, not to lose focus on them. At the same time, we must know how to motivate and encourage others to care about what matters most.

- Reach the goal in a long and persistent way, without burning the stage. Take time to build lasting relationships based on how you treat each other with sincerity and respect.

- Know how to use your senses and sixth sense to create an advantage in communication. At the same time, we must serve everyone with a warm and loving heart.

- Know how to create a happy, friendly working environment, so that everyone has the opportunity to develop their full potential.

- Sacrifice... people often use the term servant leader to describe talented leaders. It sounds cliché, but it is actually very true. They are people who are dedicated, loyal, and eager to serve others.[2]

♥ What is mindful leadership?

Many people still find it strange to talk about mindful leadership. In fact, a mindful leader is understood to be a simple leader with a calm mind, handling work wisely with a civilized and right attitude. In other words, the leader practices mindfulness to master himself in every thought, control his emotions, and become a friendly leader with empathy and tolerance and a compassionate heart.

In the early 1970s, mindfulness meditation was introduced and studied by scientists in the West.[3] Many studies on the benefits of mindfulness meditation have been spread widely, and many people started putting meditation practice on the menu every day. Mindfulness meditation provides leaders with a way of incorporating mindfulness into all aspects of their lives, allowing them to reduce stress, maintain awareness and focus, and to make highly effective decisions both personal and professional.[4]

Many people are concerned about the value of mindfulness meditation because they think the method is new age and nuanced from a particular religion. In fact, mindfulness meditation is a simple method, and is practiced without any form of religion, even though it is known in Buddhist nuances. But the essence of mindfulness meditation is non-religious and is a method you can practice anytime and anywhere, without the need for a ritual or the requirement to sit in the meditation hall of a Buddhist institute.

Many distinguished leaders have practiced mindfulness and have had great success, including Phil Jackson, the basketball coach at the Los Angeles Lakers, the champion team of the National Basketball Association (NBA). Phil Jackson was a mindfulness meditation practitioner. Many CEOs practice mindfulness meditation with great success such as: Robert Shapiro, former CEO of Monsato; William George, member of the supervisory board of Goldman Sachs Group; William Ford, president of Ford Motor Company; Steve Jobs, the late co-founder of Apple;

Robert Stiller, president of Green Mountain Coffee Roaster.

For decades, the world's leading technology corporations such as Apple, Google, Amazon, Yahoo, Intel, etc. have been applying mindfulness techniques to develop awareness leadership skills for employees. In 2007, Google started calling employees to practice mindfulness meditation. They invited Zen teachers Thich Nhat Hanh,[5] Dr. Jon Kabat-Zinn,[6] and many other speakers to share mindfulness meditation with their employees. In 2012, Google developed a program called Search Inside Yourself (SIY).[7] The purpose of this program is to apply mindfulness meditation to develop wisdom that is practical and accessible, resulting in a peaceful and friendly world in which everyone feels connected and acts with a compassionate heart. Currently (2020), more than 50,000 people have participated in the SIY program in more than 150 cities and 50 countries around the world.

Mindfulness leadership is a tool for success, keeping happiness in personal and family life. Leaders play a very important role in serving the community. Their attitude has a great influence on others, many people depend on the talent of the leader.

♥ Why must leaders practice mindful awareness?

The fact that every leader must confront in the management process is that he or she is subject to considerable pressure from many sides. They have a great deal of work to deal with, a lot of decisions that must be made promptly and rightly, and their minds can be caught up in this pressure. In addition, the continuous meetings, project after project, trying to achieve the planed goals that the company has set out, places a great deal of expectation of leadership skills on them as well as others. They put most of their energy into work, inversely proportional to the balance in life. Many mental health phenomena appear like stress, insomnia, inability to control emotions, and depressive symptoms.

In particular, in a constantly changing world, leadership becomes stressful because of an unpredictable future. To succeed, leaders need more time to think of important strategies. A successful leader needs to meet the basic elements like focus and insight in decision making; creativity in managing change within business; always be warm with customers and their staff; and also have courage to go their own way.

Thus, a leader who practices mindfulness will improve himself, resolve conflicts skillfully, be able to inspire, and be creative at work. A concept proposed by McIntyre and Green[8] as a quality feature of long-term sustainability, includes four aspects.

The I quadrant: At the personal level, the leaders need to develop good qualities such as compassion, tolerance, patience, forgiveness, empathy for themselves and others.

The It quadrant: At the audience aspect, the leader participates and acts brightly in resolving mild conflicts, negotiating techniques, fluent dialogue, restorative justice, conciliate conflict, adaptive and open

The We quadrant: At the subject aspect, the leader always knows how to motivate and inspire, allowing communities to unite and build organizations to share knowledge, activities, discussion forums and a lifetime of practice in spiritual life.

The Its quadrant: At the object aspect, the leader always listens, allowing one to turn theory into practice, implement creative and groundbreaking ideas.

Success of the leader requires calmness, harmony, kindness, and creativity. Four methods of mindfulness for lasting peace are the key to success if applied in the field of leadership. As a company wants to implement a new project, the leader needs to be heard (ITS) and support to contribute ideas during project implementation (IT). After summarizing the ideas to make a decision (I), and finally all actively take action after the ideas have been approved (WE).

Maintaining the above four backgrounds with the leader's mindfulness practice will make a breakthrough that leads to success in the work from individual to the nation: resolving conflicts at an individual level – in a sense next to *The I quadrant*. Resolve conflicts at the level of the people around you – with *The We quadrant*. Conflict resolution in organizations that share common aspirations – by *the It quadrant* aspect. Conflict resolution in a community – by the aspect *the Its quadrant*.

Practicing mindfulness helps you master the emotions. When you control your emotions, you have the ability to control yourself, and become a successful leader. Daniel Goleman has inspired leaders to embrace skills and control emotions. Goleman's work sparked a revolution in emotional intelligence that was quickly applied and used by corporations around the world in the role of mindfulness leadership. He gave five keys to reap the success of the leader.[9]

Self-awareness, that is, a leader knows about mastering emotions, hobbies, inherent energy, and intuitiveness in problem solving.

Managing emotional: Always know how to turn compulsion into choices, managing impulses, resources, and intuition. In other words, giving emotions to them is appropriate as an ability to build self-awareness at work in a harmonious manner.

Motivating oneself, knowing goals are essential to pay attention, motivation and creativity are very important for the majority, in accordance with the overall value, motivate leaders to commit.

Recognizing emotions in others, also known as empathy, is the awareness of the feelings of others in order to have a harmony in cultivating connection and mutual trust in the leader.

Handling relationships, which means cultivating skills in communication, especially listening, skillful participation in handling conflicts with compassion and responsibility.

If we want to manage our emotions, the most important factor is practicing mindfulness. Practicing is valuable to show the right attitude which leads to action. Because when you practice mindfulness every day it becomes a habit, then builds as a timeless memory, which is even more beneficial than habit. Your practice has the ability to transform a weak life into a strong person, who thinks, acts, and helps others.

Leaders really need awareness to have the balance, build strength from within such as developing mindfulness, concentration, wisdom, and cognitive ability. Thereby helping them reduce stress and solve work problems effectively. Thus, mindfulness meditation is not merely a practice for retreatants in deep forest monasteries, but mindfulness meditation is a very scientific practice applied to the field of leadership. With strong growth, many people are mindful of mindfulness for its practical benefits.

♥ Maintaining mindfulness in leaderships

All phenomena are constantly changing, even human consciousness changes every moment. Therefore, leaders need to practice mindfulness to cultivate peace, tranquility, and balance in their work and life. Leadership is closely related to the values of success, peace, and happiness. Therefore, the leader himself needs to maintain a mindfulness practice to change the desired social community. The leader's model of maintaining a balance includes the following virtues:

Intelligence or insight is positively related to leadership. Many studies have shown that leaders need to have ability in using effective language, awareness and reasoning to handle every job. It's good that leaders use intelligence in problem solving, but they also need to be kind to their subordinates. In other words, a leader shouldn't be too different from his subordinates. If the leader shows a difference from the followers, it can backfire on the relationship between the two. Highly capable leaders may have difficulty communicating with followers because they are preoccupied or because their ideas are too advanced for their followers to accept.

Self-confidence is one of the traits a leader needs. Self-confidence is a person's ability, knowledge, and aptitude. Leaders who show confidence include a sense of self-esteem and confidence in decisions to make a difference. Leadership in this quality greatly influences others and allows those around them to feel reassured that leadership's efforts to inspire others are fit and appropriate.

Determination is a character that leader must have in their work. Determination includes the desire to complete the work as quickly and effectively as possible. It includes traits such as initiative, perseverance, dominance, and assertiveness. People with determination are willing to assert themselves, be proactive and able to persevere in facing obstacles or difficulties. Determination includes showing dominance at times, not only in situations that are geared towards goals, but also being patient in overcoming failure.

Integrity is one of the most important characteristics of a leader. Integrity is a quality of honesty and trustworthiness. Those who abide by the strong principles and responsibility for their actions are manifesting integrity. Leaders with integrity will inspire and create belief in others, because they can be trusted to put what they say into actions. Basically, integrity is a reliable quality that does what is right, good, and fair.

Sociability; the last important characteristic for leaders is being sociable. A leader with sociable character is a person who tends to seek relationships with others in a peaceful, calming, and pleasant manner. Harmony is friendliness, politeness, and skillfulness in diplomacy. Moreover, sociable leaders are very concerned about the well-being and benefits of others, always creating cooperative relationships with subordinates.

In order to have the above qualities, a leader needs to maintain mindfulness in his or her daily life.

In a laptop with the battery drained of its power, all functions will be congested. The iPhone that runs out of battery power cannot communicate with anyone. Leaders need to shine the light of mindfulness on all actions, thoughts, and problems. A successful leader cannot lack mindfulness. Mindfulness, just like the battery power, has the role of enabling functions to connect smoothly and clearly in every task of daily life.

♥ The benefit of mindful leaders

The application of mindfulness into the field of leadership helps us develop ourselves as a long-term sustainable leader. The first thing is that we will feel is calm and relax. Evidence-based mindfulness interventions are growing and can be a preventing tool for leaders, such as reducing stress, anxiety or other forms of psychological suffering, and also increasing ability to focus, improving memory, increasing control over emotions and quality of thinking.[10] Maintaining practice will minimize worries and promote a life that appears to be full of contentment and satisfaction. You will have positive thoughts and easily handle difficulties or challenges such as economic crisis or professional hardship. While the difficulty persists, you still have the energy to calm it down. Awakened energy is very important for you to accept what is happening and make the right decisions. Marc Lesser's experience[11] shows the practical benefits of being a leader with mindfulness practice.

Love to work. Start with inspiration and be aware of what is most important. Always acknowledge and cultivate the inspiration, insight, and the most sincere intention.

Do the work. Practice mindfulness meditation daily. Learn how to react appropriately in your workplace and in your life.

Avoid being an expert. Let go of the mindset that you are always right. Always opening your heart to except good things, beauty, and listening to correct imperfections.

Connect to our pain. Never run away with grief or failure, instead face it strongly as part of your life. When you recognize pain, you will find a way to heal it easily.

Connect the pain of others as yourself. When you feel your pain, you have the ability to sympathize and share your pain with others. You are showing a deep connection of responsibility not only in work but also in people and life.

Depending on many other elements. Let go of the sense of false independence of the arbitrary person, always empowering and receptive to empowering others to promote the dynamism of healthy organizations and sustainable development.

Keep making it simpler. A mindset of scarcity is a negative of leadership style, as opposed to always cultivating openness, exchanging ideas, and learning from each other. The experience of mindfulness practice helps a leader to be simple in all matters.

Research on leadership behavior shows that, on average, 47% of the time of a day the mind wanders, 70% cannot focus in meetings. Meanwhile, the leader always has to handle the dense workload, has to make many decisions, thus the need for concentration is extremely necessary. Mindfulness meditation has the power to help solve this problem. The essence of meditation is being aware of the integrity of every second, every minute of life, being in contact with the actual moment, things that are really happening around us. When we practice this skill, we will always simplify things by focusing on each thing we are doing, instead of always worrying about the future or regretting past things. We will know how to focus on only one thing at a time, know the direction of our thinking about the present, not be distracted by the surrounding elements. That means we can control and improve the quality of our thoughts and choose the desired thoughts.

Moreover, when you practice meditation regularly, your mind will find a state of stillness, the flow of thoughts will be clearly separated, thereby enhancing the ability to analyze from many objective aspects, to offer more informed and precise decisions.

We can be a good strategic leader but still be overwhelmed by negative emotions, which means that we lose control of our communication, words, attitudes, or behaviors. On the journey of transformation to become a mindful leader, by practicing meditation, we will learn to look deep inside ourselves, thereby gaining self-understanding, self-awareness, and strengthen the ability to resolve negative emotions. We will be able to clearly see how emotions work, observing emotions from when they appear, change, and disappear. Then we will know how to tame negative emotions, help our self to return and maintain a positive state, creating energy to calmly handle all jobs.

Success is not the end, failure also is not the end. The important thing is the courage to keep going forward. Courage only comes from the ability to deeply understand, to strongly believe in one's self, thereby developing confident energy and bravery before events overwhelm the situation.

We can completely create energy just by controlling the quality of our thoughts and maintaining positive emotions and peace. The average person will have an average of 50,000 thoughts per day, and when worried, stressed, or angry, the number of thoughts is much greater. Mindfulness meditation is not a state of thoughtlessness, but fewer thoughts of more quality, leading to greater control over the runaway mind.

Neuroscience concludes that during meditation we make new neural connections, setting positive and simple thoughts. Meditation is a state of experiencing feelings of peace, love, happiness, etc. That is why positive thinking will create positive emotions, and the quality of thoughts will intensify.

We may hear the word mindfulness many times and know about mindfulness, but we may not feel its true meaning without practicing mindfulness meditation. Practicing mindfulness every day helps us to be stable, and when our attention is steady, our mind becomes awake instead of rattled or hijacked.

Leadership with mindfulness is simply being awake in every decision. Mindfulness is like a spotlight, illuminating streams into the mind and shaping the brain. Therefore, developing greater control over your attention is probably the most powerful way to reshape your brain which is your mind.[12]

The experience of those who apply mindfulness to leadership shows many benefits such as 1/ being more focused and calm; 2/ improving time management; 3/ improving decision making; 4/ being able to improve predictions and better serve the needs of stakeholders; 5/ decreasing the likelihood of facing a conflict; 6/ improving team working efficiency; 7/ effectiveness in being creative and inspiring at work; 8/ product manufacturing efficiency; 9/ ready to absorb stress among individuals; and 10/ willing and patient to suffer frustration and procrastination.[13] Mindfulness meditation provides a stable energy for leadership benefits, including in two personal aspects, the leadership aspect and the relationship aspect with peers.

On a personal level: Practicing meditation helps your brain regenerate to focus and be happier. An improved immune system, and lower blood pressure. A healthy heart, chronic pain relief and ability to manage it better, reduce anxiety and better in handling stress. Improve memory, ability to learn, manage emotions, and improve awareness.

In terms of relationships with colleagues: Improve the effectiveness of the team, including more effective meetings with significantly shorter time. Improve team performance and less misunderstandings. Increase your ability to identify what is the basis for most conflicts and arrive at a win-win conclusion. Individuals and teams with innovation, greater inspiration, collaboration, and common problem solving smoothly. Increase communication within and between teams. Increase the ability to anticipate and serve customers' needs, compassion and greater empathy. Higher productivity at all levels of the organization.

On the organizational side: Leadership with mindfulness practices enhances creativity, increases personal resilience and the ability to maintain performance, judge and make better decisions. Improve focus on the task, enhance concentration, and make it more effective. Capacity to work on multiple projects because of the ability to focus on one task at a time, thus becoming much more efficient and effective. Manage your time, improve your ability to solve problems by seeing situations more clearly. Improve skills for more effective coaches or advisers. Better handle stressful situations and work more effectively under pressure. Increase the ability to listen to others and use valid feedback, an ability to predict and serve the needs of customers.

8.

PRACTICE MINDFULNESS IN PRISON

In recent years, I have had the opportunity to volunteer teaching meditation for prisoners. In the process of volunteering, I have a lot of joy because I have partly helped the prisoners relieve the sadness, loneliness, and remorse in prison. Inspired by my own experience in the practice, mindfulness meditation can bring joy and happiness to everyone. In this chapter, I would like to share the needs and benefits of mindfulness meditation in prisoners' lives.

♥ Prison life

The prison is a place where the doors are always closed with many locks, where police take turns patrolling and guarding secrets. Inside, prisoners are not free to move, all acts of eating, sleeping, resting ... are controlled by police officers. Screams are heard in the cramped rooms filled with people, the sound of the iron doors opening and closing, the old air-conditioning sounding like trains. Such terrible conditions greatly affect the nerves and minds of prisoners.

Surveys show that of the two million people behind bars in US prisons, 90 percent are men; one in 147 U.S. residents is in jail or under house arrest. Among them, African Americans are seven times more numerous than whites. Among Hispanic men between the ages of twenty and thirty, four percent are in prison. More than 40 percent of prisoners have not completed high school.[1] This shows that the prison is a clear reflection of the racist and class structure that unified nations want to pretend does not exist.

In the United States (1998), the national budget for construction and prison costs has increased from

US $500 million to US $31 billion per year. One in 50 children in the United States now has one parent in prison. More and more young black men are in jail instead of going to universities.[2]

According to the data of the David Lynch Foundation (2020), the United States has the highest crime rate compared to other countries in the world and that rate has increased steadily since the 1980s to the present. There are more than two million four hundred thousand individuals in prison. State spending on repairing has quadrupled over the past 20 years, ranking it as the second fastest growing budget, reaching $52 billion annually. The cost of imprisoning an inmate is estimated at US $65,000 per year, higher than the average income of a US citizen.[3]

Loneliness and sadness are a result of being without close relatives. So much sorrow appears in the mind, happy and sad memories have been experienced in life. Frequently asked questions of an inmate entering the prison for the first time are: How can I survive this mentally, physically, and spiritually? How can I endure this harsh environment in prison? How can I experience the sense of control when I seem completely helpless?

The prison is a place of suffering, violence, noise, hatred; an environment that is not the same as the outside world.

♥ Religious in U.S. prisons

The mood of a prisoner is like a traveler drifting in the middle of a vast ocean, desperately in need of a float to hold on to a spiritual life in prison. Many inmates wrote letters asking to practice mindfulness. Many chaplains of religious traditions such as Christian, Muslim, and Judaism have entered prison to teach the prisoners.

One of the pioneers who brought Buddhist thought to guide the prisoners was Reverend Hogen Fujimoto. Prisoners in Texas wrote to Fujimoto, a Shin Buddhist minister in San Francisco. Fujimoto began introducing Buddhism to American prisoners between 1963 and 1979.[4] Around the same time, in Washington state, Dhammacharu Aryadaka was the first Buddhist chaplain to serve part-time at the prison. Despite this, religious discrimination persists against Buddhism on the part of American prison administrators and clerical bureaucracy,[5] so teaching mindfulness meditation in prisons is still difficult. In September 2000, President Bill Clinton signed a compromise law, called the Religious Liberty Protection Act,[6] and everyone in the United States had the right to follow or not follow any religion, depending on each person's wishes. This law opens the opportunity for those who want to teach meditation and Buddhist teachings in prisons without being deterred and feeling discriminated against.

In recent decades, many Buddhist monks and Buddhist chaplains have brought meditation into prisons. Reverend Kobai Scott Whitney,[7] a Buddhist chaplain in the Washington Department of Corrections, has actively brought Buddhist ideas into prison to help prisoners heal stress, change their moods, and renew their lives. At present, there are many Vietnamese Buddhist monks who have quietly brought meditation and Buddhist ideas to the prisoners, which is a Bodhisattva's wish to save sentient beings. When I taught meditation in prison as a volunteer, I used to tell myself that guiding mindfulness meditation in prison is a blessing, a reward that I wish to contribute in my life. When interacting with people in the prison, I found that among them there was no shortage of warm, gentle, intelligent, patient, kind-hearted people, loving people and friendly faces in this unfortunate environment. This makes me feel the deep faith in the teachings of the Buddha, that inside the depths of every human being are the seed of saints, seeds of enlightenment, turning around to the shore. Above all, when I feel the joy of the prisoners practicing mindfulness meditation, it also encourages me to practice mindfulness meditation more for myself.

♥ Why should mindfulness meditation to be put into prison?

It is as the time is set by default, when I have just finished signing in at the security office, Mr. King,[8] a permanent resident in his early twenties, and also a longtime mindful meditation practitioner, graciously came to accept the lotus hand, hello Master! Then he laughed and laughed happily until police officers came to open the door to the meditation practice room. While waiting for the other members to come, King told me about his practice of meditation in the early morning and the night before he went to bed.

King practiced according to the exercises that I instructed each time during meditation according to the method of mindfulness of breathing, with three steps:

Balance body

Put yourself in a comfortable, stable and firm sitting position. Sit upright, relaxed. Imagine sitting like a mountain, stable and firm, supported by mother earth. Check that the head is held comfortable on the spine, with the chin slightly lowered. Close your eyes or place them gently at a point of view in front of you. Relax our face and smile gently on our lips.

Sit with a comfortable feeling on the chair, feet touching the floor, keeping your back straight. Resting the body, feeling a sense of support from the ground below.

Balance breaths

Gently ring the bell three times to start the practice. Be conscious with the in and out breath, watching the breath from beginning to end, without being distracted. The practice during meditation, I learned from my respected teacher a few years ago, continue to apply when I meditate, and I shared with my friends in the prison.[9]

After the first two lines are read, two keywords follow, each being read with the corresponding in and out breath. Allow a few breaths in and out of each keyword:

Breathing in, I know I'm breathing in / In
Breathing out, I know I'm breathing out / Out

There is no need to change anything, just to perceive the breath naturally becoming deeper and slower. Allow your mind and body to feel calm and relaxed.

Breathing in, I feel calm in my body / Calm
Breathing out, I smile / Smile

Or:

Breathing in, I feel calm / Calm
Breathing out, I feel ease / Ease

Allow ourselves to be fully aware of the present moment and realize the conditions that make it a great moment.

Breathe in, I dwell in the present moment / Present moment
Breathe out, I know it is a wonderful moment / Wonderful moment

Balance mind

When one begins to dwell in samadhi, one observes the breath in and out consciously, maybe three minutes or five minutes, then lets go of the breath so that the mind can rest in concentration. However, the mind often thinks about the past, yesterday, or last week. When thought arises and mindfulness is perceived, do not following those lines of thought, immediately returning to the breath, practicing like that until those lines of thoughts disappear. When there are no more misleading thoughts, the mind becomes pure, clear, and the true mind appears, seeing clearly.

The prisoners practice very seriously, because of the empty mood that brings prisoners to religion, the spiritual field that has never been practiced in their religious tradition. Many people have fallen in love with the technique of mindfulness meditation. Because the method of mindfulness of breathing is very simple and can help them release stress, anxiety, and sadness.

A friend of King, Mr. Tom, shared that whenever he felt uneasy because the sorrow of the past raged and ripped his mind, he immediately found a place to sit still, close his eyes, take a deep breath, watch the breath come in from the nose to the end, feel the abdomen expand, then watch the breath come out from the beginning to the end, feeling the belly go down. He practiced like that and within a few minutes all negative emotions subsided. After saying this, he bowed his head and said, thank you, teacher, for giving me a talisman to save lives.

That gives us brilliant experiences to see that the Buddha's teachings are wonderful. If we are diligent in our practice, there will be peace and happiness immediately, so we call the teachings of the Buddha very holy, good, and great when starting out, great in the middle and great till the end.[10] Thus, if one has the practice of the Buddha's teachings, he or she has the experience of liberating all ties, rather than having to practice for six months, a year or ten years to be effective. It should be said that the Buddha's teachings are well-proclaimed, the Dhamma practice of wandering or the phenomenon of wandering in Sanskrit, DristaDhamma sukhavihara, means happiness in the present moment; it means practicing the Buddha's teachings in daily life, leaving greed and ignorance, burning the afflictions, to attain peace and liberation right in this life, now and here.

Right now, at this moment we begin to practice conscious breathing, the mind will be still, we will taste the taste of happiness, bliss, and liberation during practice, without waiting for days, months, or years. The practice of mindfulness meditation is to have joy while sitting in meditation, and not to expect to be a saint or to attain the level of a bodhisattva.

When I explained the purpose of practicing mindfulness meditation, we learned to observe ourselves. Consciousness of the breath going in and out, or being mindful of the sound of the school clock, eases the mind's endless thoughts. Letting the body and mind relax, it helps us to see ourselves better and to see all things better.

Jake, the cheerful and outgoing person, said, when practicing the meditation, he thought after he got out of jail, he would want to have a useful job, he would write a memoir talking about the practice of meditation at the time he is here in jail.

I advised Jake that if he wanted to write a good memoir and help many people know about the benefits of mindfulness meditation, he should practice every day to feel that peace…then his writing would become extremely valuable.

I wrote the word **RAIN** on the board, then explained the meaning of the word relating to the practice of mindfulness meditation. Rain…. the usual meaning is refresh, new, because of water pouring down, the trees are green and sprout. In places where the weather is clearly defined by four seasons, when the snowstorms of the winter season come to an end and sky turns to spring, the weather starts to get sunny and warmer. After a rain, the trees flush with young green shoots. The rain makes spring come from the dry branches.

Zen masters use the word **RAIN** to talk about the benefits of mindfulness meditation practice, such as water from the rain to the plants. Rain in the sense of meditation is to water the seeds of awareness, love, understanding, forgiveness, tolerance, patience, and generosity. When these elements are born, you always live in joy, happiness, liberation, and enlightenment.

The letters that make up **RAIN** have special meanings in practicing mindfulness meditation such as:

R – Recognize what is happening in the present moment. Know what is happening in the present moment. Now is the miraculous moment of life, all we can do is only in the present time. We want to transform suffering, ignorance, ignite afflictions, eradicate craving, and these can only happen at this moment. And we want to be in contact with peace, happiness, nirvana, and liberation in this moment, not at any other time. Practicing mindfulness brings the mind back to the body. When the mind is clear, you can come into contact with the mystery of peace and happiness now and here.

A – Allow / Accept life to be just as it is, accept what we have and what we are. We have the right to dream, to have great and beautiful dreams. But if we are not awake to enjoy what we have, then it is like a sleepwalking person. Meditation will help wake us up from a deep sleep of unconscious mechanical actions. From there we can truly live and can use all the abilities of consciousness and potential.

I – Investigate with kindness, touch on kindness within. For successful mindfulness meditation practice, we need patience. Because in the process of monitoring the breath going in and out, sometimes there are many challenges, because it is not always possible to maintain concentration during the sitting meditation period. We need to be kind to ourselves, that is to be patient when losing mindfulness in a cycle of counting in and out of breaths from one to ten, because there are distractions of ambition interfering with harassment. Giving awareness, smiling, patience, kindness to yourself, to keep coming back to counting the breath from one, so that you will be exposed to the kindness inside you. Kindness does not mean being naive, foolish, or silly. Kindness is the greatest power in the world. It means stepping forward with pure confidence with a true perception that we must be very kind and to put the needs of others as equal to our own.

N – Non-identification – This experience is part of being human; It was not just me. When we meditate, we have the opportunity to experience the observation of the body in the body, the observation of feeling in feeling, the observation of mind in mind, and the observation on objects of mind in object of mind, of realizing that all that makes us human are earth, water, wind, fire. Thus, this person, this form is made up of non-human factors. We live in this world which cannot exist independently, but depends on many other factors and conditions, called inter-being.[11] The word Inter, meaning there is an intimate relationship between one and the other; being, means the subjective and objective aspects of the present, that is, what is present and what is happening. Thus, inter-being can express in a concept that all phenomena are highly interrelated. In the world of discrimination, things are outside, like a cup of tea outside a mountain river, a mountain river outside the cup of tea. In the world of meditation, the cup of tea is found in the mountain river, and the mountain river is in the teacup. Looking deep into the cup of tea we see there is earth, water, fire, space, time, and many other things, all phenomena in the universe are present in the cup of tea. The one that contains the many and the many that contains the one is called inter-being.[12] It should be said that in a particle of dust are countless Buddhas. So our real job is to care, protect, love, and benefit each other.

Jake has repeated the words inter-being over and over again with joy and a happy smile, seeming to have realized something while learning and practicing mindfulness meditation.

♥ The result of mindfulness meditation practice for prisoners

The bell is rung three times to signal the end of the meditation practice. Invite everyone to breathe in and out deeply three times. Breathe deeply into the blood so that the blood follows the breath to circulate throughout the body. Breathe out so much anxiety, stress, and sadness, follow your breath out. Then open your eyes, smile, lips rubbed together for 30 seconds, then gently massage the face, head, shoulders.

Sharing time…. you have the opportunity to share what you feel after meditating, what is happening in the body and mind and how it has transformed.

King shared that meditation practice helps to relax the body and mind, watching the breath helps my mind no longer thinking about the past. The truly mysterious bell brought me back to the present moment, helping me to listen to my mind and begin to transform an unwholesome mind. My mind felt light and serene like a deer walking slowly on a green grass hill, watching a stream gurgling along the hill. The wounds in my mind seemed to be gone, and I felt very peaceful and happy in the present moment. I want to sit here because I am enjoying a peaceful energy, a great feeling.

Tom shared that, after I practiced mindfulness meditation, it seemed that the mind that flew like a monkey in me was calmed down, and my body was also relieved of old wounds. What I feel is a miracle in meditation is that only using conscious breath in and out can relax the body and mind. Then I release the mind, listen to the mind and tell the mind that I am here to cleanse the mind of anxiety and sorrow, and to begin living a miraculous moment right now and here. No more sorrow and pain, but I have true peace. Mr. Tom added that I actually had a religious practice when I was a child, often followed my parents to go to church on the weekends, but now when facing difficulties in my life, the religion I'm practicing cannot solve it or resolve the pain in me. Through breathing, my mind made my body relax. That is the miracle of being awakened by healing energy.

Meanwhile, a person sitting opposite me said in an overflowing emotion, I felt ashamed of the drug and drug acts… that's why I am here. I cannot take care of my two young children right now.

Max, a young man of less than 25-year olds, said, I've really changed a lot since practicing mindfulness meditation. I used to be very short-tempered, easily angered and ready to fight. Mindfulness meditation helped me to treat my temper and it helped me a lot. I learned to control my temper and control my emotions. I find myself more focused and less irritated. Sometimes during the day, I would sit down, close my eyes, pay attention to my breathing. Meditation and the Buddha's teachings changed my life. I hope all of you in jail come to meditate, as it has many benefits.

There is a lot of sharing about the results of mindfulness meditation practice in prison. What I find most interesting is that regardless of whether the elderly or young people, people who suffer a lot or suffer little, when there is a chance to come into contact with mindfulness meditation, there is a transformation from suffering to peace of mind

There are many prisoners who are fascinated by the benefits of meditation in the midst of a difficult situation during prison time, who have had the opportunity to look back at themselves and desire to live well, as well as renew their lives. Practicing meditation means returning to the inside, and everyone inside has the holy quality. But because of difficult living conditions, not being educated, and growing up in an unhealthy environment, they chose the wrong path and committed a sin.

However, in my experience of instructing mindfulness meditation in prison, I met some very excited inmates. Kent, 28 years old, asked, teacher, can meditation teach flying or invisibility? I ask, why do you like to learn to fly or stealth, for what reason? I want to run away from this place, Kent answered. I laughed and said, are you joking? Practicing mindfulness meditation helps him to know himself, his conception of life, and to realize the integrity of every second and every minute of life. That is, if you practice mindfulness and liberate your mind from attachment, you will have joy wherever you live. If he flies out of here, can he escape the police hunt. Kent laughed!

There are many people who live in a favorable environment where their minds are bound, so being unable to enjoy what they have is like being in a prison. In the old days, when Buddha was still in the world, the notorious bandit Angulimāla,[13] was a brutal hunter, making the people in the village of Kosala fearful. Because of the appearance of this bandit, everyone in the village, the city, and the country are no longer peaceful. Angulimāla killed one at a time, then cut off their index fingers to make into a rosary. This notorious bandit believed that if he strikes a thousand fingers, he will go to heaven.

One morning, like every other day, the Blessed One was on his way to Savatthi temple to beg for alms and preach to the public. Angulimāla saw the Buddha and chased in the hope of taking his life to get a thousand fingers and fulfill his terrible wish. Angulimāla chased forever but could not catch up with the Buddha, the bandit cried out, "Hey Gotama, stop!".

Buddha leisurely replied: "I have already stopped, Angulimāla! Please stop!" Angulimāla seemed to go on a rampage and shouted, "What are you saying? Why are you stopping now?" The Buddha replied, "For all beings, I have let go of the malice with the sword, with the war cane and with the bow. I have truly stopped for a long time. And you are sowing hatred and causing death and grief for many others. Hey Angulimāla, stop it." Hearing such instructions, the robber dropped his sword and bowed his head and became the enlightened being.

The awakened energy eradicates the cruel sword and the atrocities of murderers. When the awakened energy exists, all evil will fall and bow to make way for the beauty of holiness in every human being. Each of us has the seeds of a wicked corpse like Angulimāla, and everyone has the nucleus of awakening and enlightenment like Buddha.

The statistics show us that more than fifty percent of the prisoners released return to prison within three years because of committing a crime.[14] This shows that the bad habits are not easily changed, it takes a great will to hope to heal.

The mindfulness method is very simple, but to succeed requires great effort and a serious discipline. It is also easy to understand, because we have to deal with a very strong sense of forgetfulness, the unconscious habits in us. These energies are very strong and they come from within. So sometimes we need a determination as well as trying just to maintain our practice, as well as to capture the present moment. But it is very satisfying, because it helps us to come into contact with new aspects of life that we have lost because we refused to see.[15]

The environment in the prison is very bad. It can increase the illness and take the lives of many people in it. The light of mindfulness meditation shines in the darkness of prison, lighting up hope for prisoners to have the opportunity to awaken to renew their lives, live peacefully, and become useful people later when they reunite with family.

Practicing mindfulness meditation is like practicing and learning the art of life, or in other words, walking the path of life. The space and the time of that path are spreading right now and here, and at any moment in which we truly live consciously. Mindfulness meditation is literally a way of living fully, rather than a method. Because the practice of mindfulness meditation opens up a path of listening, love, tolerance, and forgiveness; a path to peace, happiness, and harmony to live in a harmonious, friendly and miraculous way.

Sit still, monitor your breath for a period of 10 minutes, or 20 minutes, or 30 minutes twice a day. The benefits of meditation can open a way of life for prisoners, reduce stress and anxiety, and change the attitude towards honesty while in prison and reduce recidivism by more than 30 percent.[16] May we all live in peace and inherit the equal rights of human life.

9.

METHOD OF MINDFUL BREATHING PRACTICE

The method of practicing mindfulness is very simple. You can find a quiet, appropriate place during the day. There are many ways to sit the body. You can practice with full lotus or half lotus or burmese position. If sitting on a chair, drop your feet to the ground, sit straight with a long spine. Keep your hands folded, resting on your legs just below your stomach or unfolded resting on your knees. The sitting posture is firm, relaxed, gentle, and eyes closed.

Here is a sitting meditation mindfulness practice supply.

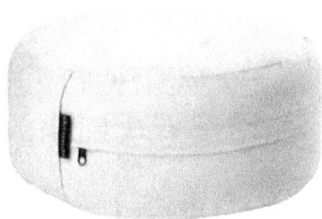

One cushion about twenty centimeters high and twenty centimeters in diameter, stuffed with kapok, soft and flexible. It should sit about ten centimeters off the ground. The cushion sizes are varied depending on the practitioner's preference.

One mat about seventy centimeters square is spread on the floor, the cushion on top.

Siting on the center of the cushion, keeping your back straight, do not lean backward or forward or swing left and right. Just sitting to achieve a comfortable and very relaxed position.

Hand position in seated meditation. The right hand is on the left, fingers on fingers. Both hands rest on the pillow or the legs. The two tips of the thumb touch lightly near the navel.

For the full lotus position put the felt foot on the right thigh and the right foot on the left thigh. Both knees should touch the mat.

For the half-lotus position put the left foot on the right thigh. Or vice versa, it depends on the practitioner's comfortable side.

Burmese Position is where your lower body is crossed with one leg folded in font of the other. It is possibly the most common posture for meditors to take and practice mindfulness breath.

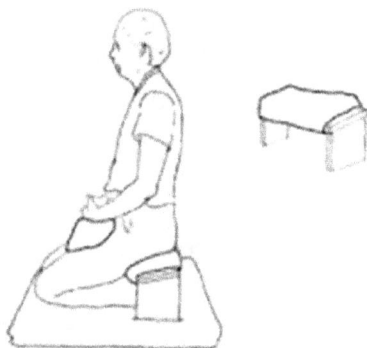

Using a meditation bench, we will simply place the bench behind and get into a kneeling position. We will slide the bench towards your behind, keep our ankles flat behind and move the bench until it is directly above our ankles. Then sit down and rest our bottom on the seat. If this does not feel comfortable, we can feel free to adjust the angle and position of the bench and our bottom until it feels right.

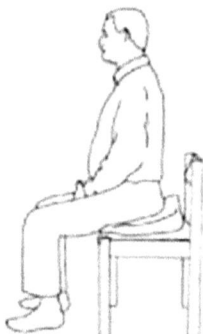

We can practice meditation on sitting on a chair if our knees don't agree with any of the positions above, or if we need a backup seat for longer meditation sessions. But we might need a thin cushion either to get our height right, or to support the lower back.

Lying down relaxation is an effective practice that helps the body stay in tune with the heart and mind. Like sitting meditation, the aim of lying down is important.... that the body and mind rest and remain as stable and still as possible. This physical stability supports the mind as it acquires and sustains a state of awareness.

Walking meditation is a very effective way to connect the body, breath, and mind. It is a way to imprint peace on the earth. Being mindful of each step as it begins and ends helps us come out of our egoistic head and back to our feet, allowing us to stop running and dwell in the present moment. It is a way to reunite the body and mind.

Focus on the breath in and out very naturally; that means paying attention to the breath without trying to make it long or short. Follow the breath in its natural rhythm. Breathe regularly and peacefully. The breath is the only object during the practice of mindfulness. Occasionally the mind is distracted and fluttering, thinking about the past or dreaming about the future. When you realize this is happening you must try to be awake and bring the mind back to the object of meditation by watching the breath coming in and out. Pay attention to areas of sensation of the breath like the flow of air on the nose or the abdomen as it rises and falls. Imagine that the breath that comes in and out is a hook. Attention is the invisible line that binds the mind to the object of mindfulness meditation, following the breath-monitoring method so the mind doesn't get distracted.

Focus your attention on the breath touching point at the nose or upper lip. If you feel uncomfortable or stressed, you can focus your attention on the area below your belly button or keep your mind in front of you. Attention during meditation must be full of three factors of mindfulness: attention, awareness, and alertness. The process of practicing mindfulness following the breathing method, progresses through the following contemplation topics:

♥ Take care of your body

Pay close attention to the breath so that you are aware of your in and out breath, long breath or short breath (in, out, long, short). Use only bare attention to the breath and clearly identify long breath in and out, or short breath in and out. Just clearly recognize the four manifestations of the breath: in / out; long / short. Be conscious of the manifestations of each breath in a specific way to keep the mind awake, not wandering, slowly reaching concentration. When the mind is calm, there is no more distraction, and the breathing becomes light.

1.

Breathing in long, he discerns, I am breathing in long;
or breathing out long, he discerns, I am breathing out long.

2.

Or breathing in short, he discerns, I am breathing in short;
or breathing out short, he discerns, I am breathing out short.[1]

A distracted mind, with difficulty concentrating, is a fairly common disease that many people encounter in society today. The mind is governed by many external factors such as work, life, and relationships, which keep the mind reeling and the lines of thought continuously flowing. There are many people who go crazy because they cannot stop their thoughts. They look to stimulants such as alcohol or sedatives with the desire to find themselves a little rest to temporarily forget the pressures and worries of life. They are engulfed in drunkenness, and the anxiety, frustration, and fear remain intact and silently attacks them with nightmares. They wake up with a tired, dull body like a lost soul.

Therefore, it is important to return to the conscious mind whenever we feel insecure in our daily lives, because it has the power to quell the flow of distracting thoughts and simultaneously awaken them so that one awakens with mindful energy. Stopping all thoughts and suspending the way of surrendering to oblivion by paying close attention to the conscious breath is an extremely important step in the spiritual life. It is truly a miraculous gift of life.

When the five aggregates of the existence do not get along well with one another, there will be conflict between family relatives such as parents, spouses, children, or in the relationship of friends, neighbors. It is a sign of insecurity in the body that leads to internal disorders. Body and mind always go hand in hand, so when the body is sick, the mind will be insecure. When there is a civil war inside, there is definitely war on the outside. So when a person often causes conflict, yelling, irritability, discomfort, anger, reproach, condemnation, he or she knows that there is a civil war within, and the mind is very poor and lacking love. Faced with such difficulties, the Buddha taught to return to the breath, to apply mindfulness to enlighten the interior, and the five aggregates will be reconciled, so that the mind is calm and conflict free. Practice exercising the third breath:

3.

He trains himself, I will breathe in sensitive to the entire body.
He trains himself, I will breathe out sensitive to the entire body.[2]

Awareness of the whole in-breath includes from the beginning, the middle, the end of the in-breath, and the whole out-breath from the beginning, the middle, and the end of the exhalation. This is an attempt to record the whole breath clearly. We rarely pay attention to parts of the body when they are painful or damaged. Sometimes we have spent ten years or fifteen years to build an image or position in life, but never took the time to be consciously aware with a warm heart of our own hand. One's hand is particularly important. If you do not love and take care of it, one day it will not work with you to aid you in achieving another wish. Psychological, physiological, and physical phenomena are all gateways to the true being.

At times, the body is here but the mind ran away somewhere else. Mindfulness invites the body, mind, and breath to become one. Initially the practice of all three things, body, mind, and breath, is not very mature, not yet smooth, but practicing for fifteen or twenty minutes we will feel light, settled, and calm. The Fourth breath:

4.

He trains himself, I will breathe in calming bodily fabrication.
He trains himself, I will breathe out calming bodily fabrication.[3]

When walking in the snow, feeling the cold, if you drink a cup of hot tea, you will feel warm. With mindfulness you can also notice the warm breath. That warm breath enters the body soothing all the cells. Practicing the fourth breath nourishes the mind's cells. This breath has brought you peace, it is a food for the mind. It is called the joy of the mystic trance meditating, which is the happiness and relaxation provided by the practice of mindfulness meditation.

♥ Feelings transformation

Practicing mindfulness meditation has the function of healing wounds and cultivating peace. Thanks to the awakened energy, we can deeply connect with the mystery of life, feel the things that heaven and earth and nature bestow on us such as white clouds, blue skies, yellow flowers, wind in the pine trees, birds singing, etc. This body is impermanent, changing every moment. Nothing is separate, and pure, but it is also very precious and mysterious. Listen to the mystery of the body in harmony with the mystery of heaven and earth as we step on the path of the white snow covered in joy. Feeling at ease and at peace when we leave the bustling city and enjoying the fresh air. When I walked out of the examination room after putting all my energy into homework and ending the school year with a joyful and gentle mood, I was able to get rid of all my anxiety. Or at the end of the week, turn off the computer and get out of the office to go home to light a scented candle in the meditation room, sit down to relax and start practicing smiling and breathing. It is the joy of practicing mindfulness, simple and close. The fifth and sixth mindful exercises:

5.

He trains himself, I will breathe in sensitive to
rapture.
He trains himself, I will breathe out sensitive to
rapture.

6.

He trains himself, I will breathe in sensitive to pleasure.
He trains himself, I will breathe out sensitive to
pleasure.[4]

Practicing mindfulness is to create joy and happiness for body and mind. This joy helps the practice to be persistent. It's like the rare relaxing moments of a weekend become extremely valuable when you know how to get rid of all tiredness and troubles after a week of study or work. This is also the time when you re-energize yourself to prepare for a new week of work/study more enthusiastically and effectively. Also, the practitioner practices the mindful breath every day to transform suffering into pleasures and nourish joy into his life. Very likely, that joy spreads to loved ones, to family and friends.

When there are feelings such as frustration because the boss is annoying, anger because our love one is not on time, fatigue after a long day of work, or anxiety because of unstable work... these initiate unsettled mental states. Whenever these unsettled feelings arise, we use mindfulness to recognize them, and be aware of the mental states that are present in us. Practicing the seventh and eighth breath:

7.

He trains himself, I will breathe in sensitive to mental fabrication.
He trains himself, I will breathe out sensitive to mental fabrication.

8.

He trains himself, I will breathe in calming mental fabrication.
He trains himself, I will breathe out calming mental fabrication.[5]

The practice of mindfulness meditation in Buddhism is established on the basis of bare attention, which means when there is joy in the mind, noting that there is joy in the mind; and when there is frustration, recognizing that in the mind there is frustration. Therefore, the meditator does not have an attitude of hatred, dispelling the state of frustration, or the attitude of love, pampering the state of well-being. The mindfulness that the Buddha taught is not to create a boundary between good and evil in the body and mind and then turn it into a battlefield fighting each other. That is not what the Buddha taught.

Instead, one who practices mindfulness meditation always uses compassionate mind to treat non-violent frustration. Using loving-kindness mind to deal with any unintended things like your own loved one.

In the light of mindfulness, the frustration will be repelled and gradually transformed. Frustration, anxiety, melancholy are some of the fifty-one sensations that constantly accompany feelings. Each feeling has its own energy. The peaceful feeling brings therapeutic energy to nourish you, while uneasy feelings bring destructive energy to destroy body and mind. Practicing mindfulness is not to fight, to destroy, but just to choose the feeling of peace and joy contained in the treasury to use, and drive the feeling of insecurity out of the mind. Feelings and mental conduct are born of the conditions. Any act of attachment, holding any feeling, whether suffering or joy, leads to suffering. The light of mindfulness energy is to recognize and then learn how to turn frustrating, unsettling energy into useful energy that nourishes the body and mind. The blissfulness that mindfulness brings is completely absent of the mind-set, just like the surface of the sea does not have a ripple to bring peace to the ships!

♥ Submission and liberation of mind

The consciousness here is to speak in general about psychological phenomena including thought, perception, imagination, discrimination, and subconsciousness. Whenever a mental phenomenon is manifested, use the mindful breath to identify it and give awareness to know its connection with other parts. Practice mindful exercises with the ninth to the twelfth breath:

9.

He trains himself, I will breathe in sensitive to the mind.
He trains himself, I will breathe out sensitive to the mind.

10.

He trains himself, I will breathe in satisfying the mind.
He trains himself, I will breathe out satisfying the mind.

11.

He trains himself, I will breathe in steadying the mind.
He trains himself, I will breathe out steadying the mind.

12.

He trains himself, I will breathe in releasing the mind.
He trains himself, I will breathe out releasing the mind.[6]

The mind is a stream of psychological phenomena that constantly change, arising and ceasing non-stop. The arising and falling of one phenomenon is related to the arising and falling away of another phenomenon. The activity of the mind is often disturbing, wandering, sometimes thinking about this, sometimes running to that, like a monkey swinging branch to branch or like a waterfall falling from above and never stopping. Contemplating to see the arising and passing away of the mind is a fairly successful practice. Because when we see the nature of mind, we can stop and not follow that whirling thought. More importantly, when we see that stream of thought, we return to the breath of consciousness to calm the mind, and when the mind is collected, and we stop thinking about it, we feel immediate peace. Because we have the ability to untie the attachments, the attachment of pain in the mind. It is a successful process of practicing mindfulness meditation.

♥ Contemplating the general truth of all Dhammas

All Dhammas are impermanent and seeing all things as impermanent is an extremely important practice. No single phenomenon exists independently, and all phenomena are subject to the same rule of impermanence. Everything is constantly moving and under the influence of one another; there is no self. To see the nature of impermanence is to see the nature of non-self, and to understand clearly the self is to start seeing nirvana. It should be said, impermanence is the gateway to selflessness, and egolessness is the door to nirvana. No-self is Nirvana. Impermanence, egolessness, and nirvana are called the three Dhamma seals, a process which goes from penetrating knowledge to breaking through the web of phenomena that enter the true being. Practicing the thirteenth breath to the sixteenth breath:

13.

He trains himself, I will breathe in focusing on inconstancy.
He trains himself, I will breathe out focusing on inconstancy.

14.

He trains himself, I will breathe in focusing on
dispassion [literally, fading].
He trains himself, I will breathe out focusing on
dispassion.

15.

He trains himself, I will breathe in focusing on
cessation.
He trains himself, I will breathe out focusing on
cessation.

16.

He trains himself, I will breathe in focusing on
relinquishment.
He trains himself, I will breathe out focusing on
relinquishment. [7]

All things are impermanent, so all phenomena have
to go through an abortive process of birth, stay,
change (decay), and death. Birth means arising; stay
is a pillar exists; decay is always changing; and death
is disappearing, no longer present. For example,
the narcissus flower blooms in the spring, persists
for a period of three or four weeks, then fades, then
disappears in the winter when the snow falls. Human
bodies, trees, houses, etc. all bear the same law of
birth and then disintegrate. In fact, even on this body,

there is impermanence every second, every minute, every day, and scientists have found that our bones produce about 2.5 million red blood cells to replace the number. Cells die in every second. [8] At the same time, feelings, perceptions, and thoughts are also born to replace old feelings, perceptions, and thoughts. This process has continuity, inheritance, and replacement, that is a transition between the old and the new. It even happens and changes faster than the cells and other physical things in the body.

Therefore, the practice of impermanence is very important in the Buddhist teachings taught by the Blessed One to the disciples, so that they might contemplate to advance on the path of practice. The ancestors also practiced by visualization:

"Formerly glowing cheeks and pink lips
Today could ashes and white bones.
Position, renown though unsurpassed,
They are but part of a long dream.
However rich and noble you are,
You are no less impermanent,
Jealousy, pride and self-clinging,
But self is always empty.
Great strength, ability and success.
But in them is no final truth.

Since the four elements come apart,
Why discriminate old from young?
Crevices erode even mountain,
More quickly the hero is dead
Black hair has hardly grown on our head
When suddenly it has turned white.
Our well-wisher has just departed
A mourner arrives on our death."[9]

Similar to the body, we also contemplate the mind. The mind can be alert and sharp in the morning and can become confused, frail, slow, late in the afternoon.

When it comes to impermanence, we often think of mourning, destruction, or ruin. But to understand deeply about impermanence, let us thank it, because thanks to impermanence disease is healed, poverty can pass, a disaster will be replaced by peace and happiness thanks to impermanence. We abandon the human condition to attain enlightenment, the attainment of saints, Buddhahood. Therefore, before the Blessed One entered Nirvana, He instructed his students that All conditioned things are of a nature to decay and we should strive on untiringly.[10] Understanding impermanence means that the mind is no longer entangled and bounded, so it can escape all suffering and reach the goal of Nirvana. "Impermanent are compounded things, prone to rise and fall, having risen, they're destroyed, their passing truest bliss."[11]

Practicing the sixteen mindfulness breaths can transform and heal the body, feelings, mind and understanding of all the Dhammas. The first four mindful exercise breaths have therapeutic powers for the body; the next four breaths are capable of caring for feelings; the next four breaths can subdue the mind; and the last four breaths help to reflect on the true nature of all Dhammas. We can apply the steps of practicing mindfulness of breathing to our daily life anytime, anywhere, while walking, standing, lying and sitting. To be fully aware may be called mindfulness practice, remembering that the breath is the key to keeping mindfulness, and the foundation of mindfulness in the present moment.

When you practice walking meditation, as you walk, every step from the time you lift your foot to the moment you put your foot down, you must notice the lifting of the foot, bringing it forward, and lowering it down. Similarly, when you are mindful while preparing to cook, you can cook food with caution; or mindful while driving, you can wait for the traffic light to take a leisurely drive.

Wake up, breathe fresh air every morning, hear the birds singing, catch the morning sun and feel the positive energy flowing into your body. Start your day with every step, every thought, every action in mindfulness.

Practicing mindfulness begins and ends right in our bodies. Practicing mindfulness means spending all our time paying attention to where we are, what is happening around us, bringing the mind back to being aware of the body and its functioning. Just being aware of the mind being on an object, that is, the mind located on a point, calms the body and mind, because our body has an internal rhythm that helps it relax if we give it a chance.

ENDNOTES

DISCOVERING MINDFULNESS

1. Kabat-Zinn, J. (2005)., *Wherever You Go There You Are*. New York: Hyperion.

2. Kabat-Zinn, J. (2013)., *Full Catastrophe Living: Using the Wisdom of Your Body and Mind to Face Stress, Pain, and Illness*. New York: Bantam.

3. Jennings, Patricia A. (2015)., *Mindfulness for Teachers: Simple Skills for Peace and Productivity in the Classroom*. New York: Norton & Company.

4. Thera, Nyanaponika A. (1998)., *The Heart of Buddhist Meditation: A Handbook of Mental Training Based on the Buddha's Way of Mindfulness.*, Kandy, Sri Lanka: Buddhist Puclication Society.

5. Thera, Nyanaponika A. (1998)., *The Heart of Buddhist Meditation: A Handbook of Mental Training Based on the Buddha's Way of Mindfulness.*, Kandy, Sri Lanka: Buddhist Puclication Society.

6. Bhikkhu Nanamoli, Bhikkhu Bodhi Translators, (1995)., *The Middle Length Discourses of the Buddha: A Translation of the Majjhima Nikaya (The Teachings of the Buddha)*. MA: Boston, Wisdom Publications. p. 941.

7. Bhikkhu Nanamoli, Bhikkhu Bodhi Translators, (1995)., *The Middle Length Discourses of the Buddha: A Translation of the*

Majjhima Nikaya (The Teachings of the Buddha). MA: Boston, Wisdom Publications. p. 145.

8. Nhat Hanh, T. (2006)., *Transformation & Healing*. California: Berkeley. p.9.

9. Freke, Timothy. (2015)., *The Wisdom of the Zen Masters*, Kindle Edition.

10. Lehrhaupt, L. & Meibert, P. (2017)., *Mindfulness-Based Stress Reduction – The MBSR Program for Enhancing Health and Vitality*, Novato, California: New World Library.

11. Lehrhaupt, L. & Meibert, P. (2017).. *Mindfulness-Based Stress Reduction – The MBSR Program for Enhancing Health and Vitality*, Novato, California: New World Library.

12. Kelley Raab. (2014)., Mindfulness, Self-Compassion, and Empathy Among Health Care Professionals: A Review of the Literature, *Journal of Health Care Chaplaincy, 20*:3, 95-108, DOI: 10.1080/08854726.2014.913876

13. Kabat-Zinn, J. (2005).. *Wherever You Go There You Are*: New York, Hyperion.

14. Nhat Hanh, T (2006)., *Transformation & Healing*: California: Berkeley. p.9.

15. Varela, Francisco J; Thompson, Evan T; Rosch, Eleanor. (2017)., *The Embodied Mind: Cognitive Science and Human Experience*, MA: The MIT Press.

BREATHE TO HEAL AND TRANSFORM

1. Buddhaghosa Bhadantacariya (Author), Bhikkhu Ñanamoli (Translator) (1995)., *The Path of Purification: Visuddhimagga*; Buddhist Publication Society; Kandy, Sri Lanka. p. 274.

2. Bhikkhu Nanamoli, Bhikkhu Bodhi Translators, (1995)., *The Middle Length Discourses of the Buddha: A Translation of the Majjhima Nikaya (The Teachings of the Buddha)*; MA: Boston, Wisdom Publications. p. 941.

3.   Bhikkhu Nanamoli, Bhikkhu Bodhi Translators, (1995)., *The Middle Length Discourses of the Buddha: A Translation of the Majjhima Nikaya (The Teachings of the Buddha)*; MA: Boston, Wisdom Publications. p. 945.

4.   Bhikkhu Nanamoli, Bhikkhu Bodhi Translators, (1995)., *The Middle Length Discourses of the Buddha: A Translation of the Majjhima Nikaya (The Teachings of the Buddha)*; MA: Boston, Wisdom Publications. p. 945.

5.   Chinese version: Xīnbùzàiyān, shì'érbùjiàn, tīng'érbùwén, shí ér bùzhī qí wèi (心不在焉, 視而不見, 聽而不聞, 食而不知 其味).

6.   Bhikkhu Nanamoli, Bhikkhu Bodhi Translators, (1995)., *The Middle Length Discourses of the Buddha: A Translation of the Majjhima Nikaya (The Teachings of the Buddha)*; MA: Boston, Wisdom Publications. p. 945.

7.   Bhikkhu Nanamoli, Bhikkhu Bodhi Translators, (1995)., *The Middle Length Discourses of the Buddha: A Translation of the Majjhima Nikaya (The Teachings of the Buddha)*; MA: Boston, Wisdom Publications. p. 945.

8.   Bhikkhu Nanamoli, Bhikkhu Bodhi Translators, (1995)., *The Middle Length Discourses of the Buddha: A Translation of the Majjhima Nikaya (The Teachings of the Buddha)*; MA: Boston, Wisdom Publications. p. 945.

9.   Bhikkhu Nanamoli, Bhikkhu Bodhi Translators, (1995)., *The Middle Length Discourses of the Buddha: A Translation of the Majjhima Nikaya (The Teachings of the Buddha)*; MA: Boston, Wisdom Publications. p. 945.

10. Bhikkhu Nanamoli, Bhikkhu Bodhi Translators, (1995)., *The Middle Length Discourses of the Buddha: A Translation of the Majjhima Nikaya (The Teachings of the Buddha)*; MA: Boston, Wisdom Publications. p. 945.

11. Bhikkhu Nanamoli, Bhikkhu Bodhi Translators, (1995)., *The Middle Length Discourses of the Buddha: A Translation of the*

Majjhima Nikaya (The Teachings of the Buddha); MA: Boston, Wisdom Publications. p. 945.

12. Bhikkhu Nanamoli, Bhikkhu Bodhi Translators, (1995)., *The Middle Length Discourses of the Buddha: A Translation of the Majjhima Nikaya (The Teachings of the Buddha)*; MA: Boston, Wisdom Publications. p. 945.

13. **Fifty-one Mental Formations**: *5 – Universals contact* includes attention, feeling, perception, volition; *5 – Particulars* includes intention, determination, mindfulness, concentration, insight; *11 – Wholesome faith* includes inner shame, shame before others, absence of craving, absence of hatred, absence of ignorance, diligence or energy, tranquility or ease, vigilance or energy, equanimity and non-harming; *6 – Primary Unwholesome* includes craving or covetousness, hatred, ignorance or confusion, arrogance, doubt or suspicion, and wrong view; *20 – Secondary Unwholesome-10 Minor Secondary Unwholesome* includes anger; resentment or enmity; concealment, maliciousness, jealousy, selfishness or parsimony, deceitfulness or fraud, guile, desire to harm, pride; *2 Middle Secondary Unwholesome* includes lack of inner shame and lack of shame before others; *8 Greater Secondary Unwholesome* includes restlessness drowsiness, lack of faith or unbelief, laziness, negligence, forgetfulness, distraction, lack of discernment; *4 – Indeterminate* includes regret or repentance; sleepiness; initial thought and sustained thought

14. Bergson, Henri. (1998)., *Evolution Creative*, Dover Publication, inc., Mineole: New York.

15. Bhikkhu Nanamoli, Bhikkhu Bodhi Translators, (1995)., *The Middle Length Discourses of the Buddha: A Translation of the Majjhima Nikaya (The Teachings of the Buddha)*; MA: Boston, Wisdom Publications. p. 945.

16. Bhikkhu Nanamoli, Bhikkhu Bodhi Translators, (1995)., *The Middle Length Discourses of the Buddha: A Translation of the Majjhima Nikaya (The Teachings of the Buddha)*; MA: Boston, Wisdom Publications. p.945.

17. Bhikkhu Nanamoli, Bhikkhu Bodhi Translators, (1995)., *The Middle Length Discourses of the Buddha: A Translation of the Majjhima Nikaya (The Teachings of the Buddha)*; MA: Boston, Wisdom Publications. p.945.

18. Bhikkhu Nanamoli, Bhikkhu Bodhi Translators. (1995)., *The Middle Length Discourses of the Buddha: A Translation of the Majjhima Nikaya (The Teachings of the Buddha)*; MA: Boston, Wisdom Publications. p. 945.

19. Bhikkhu Nanamoli, Bhikkhu Bodhi Translators. (1995)., *The Middle Length Discourses of the Buddha: A Translation of the Majjhima Nikaya (The Teachings of the Buddha)*; MA: Boston, Wisdom Publications. p. 945.

20. Bhikkhu Nanamoli, Bhikkhu Bodhi Translators, (1995)., *The Middle Length Discourses of the Buddha: A Translation of the Majjhima Nikaya (The Teachings of the Buddha)*; MA: Boston, Wisdom Publications. p. 945.

21. Nhat Hanh, Thich., (2017)., *The Other Shore, A New Translation of the Heart Sutta with Commentaries.*, California: Berkeley. p.24.

22. Nhat Hanh, Thich., (2009). *The Blooming of a Lotus, Guided Meditation for Achieving the Miracle of Mindfulness*: Massachusetts: Boston, p.98

23. Bhikkhu Nanamoli, Bhikkhu Bodhi Translators. (1995)., *The Middle Length Discourses of the Buddha: A Translation of the Majjhima Nikaya (The Teachings of the Buddha)*; MA: Boston, Wisdom Publications. p. 945.

24. Buddhaghosa Bhadantacariya (Author), Bhikkhu Ñanamoli (Translator) (1995)., *The Path of Purification: Visuddhimagga*; Buddhist Publication Society; Kandy, Sri Lanka. p. 317.

THE WAY OF MINDFULNESS

1. Bhikkhu Nanamoli, Bhikkhu Bodhi Translators. (1995)., *The Middle Length Discourses of the Buddha: A Translation of the*

Majjhima Nikaya (The Teachings of the Buddha); MA: Boston, Wisdom Publications. p. 145.

2. Nhat Hanh, T. (2006)., *Transformation & Healing, Sutra on the Four Establishments of Mindfulness*, Berkeley: California. p. 15.

3. Thera, Nyanaponika A. (1998)., *The Heart of Buddhist Meditation: A Handbook of Mental Training Based on the Buddha's Way of Mindfulness.*, Sri Lanka: Kandy, Buddhist Puclication Society. p. 33.

4. Mahasi Sayadaw (Author), Maung Tha Noe (Translator), (1991)., *Fundamentals of Vipassana Meditation*, New Jersey: Dhammachakka Meditation Center. p.139.

5. Thera, Nyanaponika A. (1998)., *The Heart of Buddhist Meditation: A Handbook of Mental Training Based on the Buddha's Way of Mindfulness.*, Sri Lanka: Kandy, Buddhist Puclication Society. p. 70.

6. Buddhaghosa Bhadantacariya (Author), Bhikkhu Ñanamoli (Translator) (1995)., *The Path of Purification: Visuddhimagga.* Sri Lanka: Kandy, Buddhist Publication Society.

7. Dalai Lama, (2005)., *The Universe in A Single Atom: The Convergence of Science and Spirituality.* Harmony: Random House.

8. Thera, Nyanaponika A. (1998)., *The Heart of Buddhist Meditation: A Handbook of Mental Training Based on the Buddha's Way of Mindfulness.* Sri Lanka: Kandy, Buddhist Puclication Society.

9. Bhikkhu Nanamoli, Bhikkhu Bodhi Translators, (1995)., *The Middle Length Discourses of the Buddha: A Translation of the Majjhima Nikaya (The Teachings of the Buddha)*; MA: Boston, Wisdom Publications. p.159.

10. K.R. Norman. (2004)., *The Word of the Doctrine*, UK: The Pāli Text Society. p. 6.

11. Nhat Hanh, T. (2010)., *The Diamond That Cuts Through Illusion*. California: Berkeley. p. 13.

12. Nhat Hanh, T. (2006)., *Transformation & Healing, Sutra on the Four Establishments of Mindfulness*. CA: Berkeley. p.32.

13. Bhikkhu Nanamoli, Bhikkhu Bodhi Translators, (1995)., *The Middle Length Discourses of the Buddha: A Translation of the Majjhima Nikaya (The Teachings of the Buddha)*; MA: Boston, Wisdom Publications. p..925.

14. Nhat Hanh, T. (2006)., *Transformation & Healing, Sutra on the Four Establishments of Mindfulness*. CA: Berkeley. p. l.95.

THE BRAIN DURING PRACTICING MINDFULNESS

1. Linden, David J. (2007). *The Accidental Mind: How Brain Evolution Has Given Us Love, Memory, Dreams, and God*. MA: Cambridge, The Belknap Press of Harvard University Press.

2. Tarrant, Jeff. (2017)., *Meditation Interventions to Rewire the Brain: Integrating Neuroscience Strategies for ADHD, Anxiety, Depression & PTSD*. WI: PESI Publishing & Media.

3. Tarrant, Jeff. (2017)., *Meditation Interventions to Rewire the Brain: Integrating Neuroscience Strategies for ADHD, Anxiety, Depression & PTSD*. WI: PESI Publishing & Media.

4. Tarrant, Jeff. (2017)., *Meditation Interventions to Rewire the Brain: Integrating Neuroscience Strategies for ADHD, Anxiety, Depression & PTSD*. WI: PESI Publishing & Media.

5. Travis, Fred & Shear, Jonathan (2010). Focused attention, open monitoring and automatic self-transcending: Categories to organize meditations from Vedic, Buddhist and Chinese traditions. *Consciousness and Cognition, Volume 19*, Issue 4, December 2010, Pages 1110–1118, doi:10.1016/j.concog.2010.01.007.

6. Siegel, Daniel (2007)., *The Mindful Brain: Reflection and Attunement in the Cultivation of Well-Being*. New York: Norton & Company.

7. Lutz, A., Dunne, J., & Davidson, R. (2007). Meditation and the neuroscience of consciousness: An introduction. In P. Zelazo, M. Moscovitch, & E. Thompson (Eds.), *The Cambridge Handbook of Consciousness (Cambridge Handbooks in Psychology)*. Cambridge: Cambridge University Press. doi:10.1017/CBO9780511816789.020

8. Tarrant, Jeff. (2017)., *Meditation Interventions to Rewire the Brain: Integrating Neuroscience Strategies for ADHD, Anxiety, Depression & PTSD*. WI: PESI Publishing & Media.

9. Inanaga, Kazutoyo. (1998)., Frontal midline theta rhythm and mental activity. *Psychiatry Clin Neurosci. 52*(6):555-66.

10. Stevens, Rosemary A. and Jr. Shapiro (2017)., *Meditation: Self-regulation Strategy and Altered State of Consciousness*: New York: Routledge.

11. Dunn, B.R., Hartigan, J.A. & Mikulas, W.L. (1999)., Concentration and Mindfulness Meditations: Unique Forms of Consciousness? *Applied Psychophysiology and Biofeedback. 24*(3): 147-165. https://doi.org/10.1023/A:1023498629385

12. Tarrant, Jeff. (2017)., *Meditation Interventions to Rewire the Brain: Integrating Neuroscience Strategies for ADHD, Anxiety, Depression & PTSD*. WI: PESI Publishing & Media. p.11.

13. Tarrant, Jeff. (2017)., *Meditation Interventions to Rewire the Brain: Integrating Neuroscience Strategies for ADHD, Anxiety, Depression & PTSD*. WI: PESI Publishing & Media. p.11.

14. Nhat Hanh, T. (2006)., *Trasformation & Healing*. CA: Berkeley, Parallax Press.

15. Tarrant, Jeff. (2017)., *Meditation Interventions to Rewire the Brain: Integrating Neuroscience Strategies for ADHD, Anxiety, Depression & PTSD*. WI: PESI Publishing & Media.

16. Tarrant, Jeff. (2017)., *Meditation Interventions to Rewire the Brain: Integrating Neuroscience Strategies for ADHD, Anxiety, Depression & PTSD*. WI: PESI Publishing & Media.

17. Tarrant, Jeff. (2017)., *Meditation Interventions to Rewire the Brain: Integrating Neuroscience Strategies for ADHD, Anxiety, Depression & PTSD*. WI: PESI Publishing & Media. p.11.

18. Lutz, Antoine; Greischar, Lawrence L; Rawlings, Nancy B; Ricard, Matthieu; Davidson, Richard J (2004), Long-term Meditators Self-induce High-amplitude Gamma Synchrony During Mental Practice. *Proceedings of the National Academy of Sciences 101* (46) 16369-16373; DOI: 10.1073/pnas.0407401101

19. Travis, Fred & Shear, Jonathan (2010). Focused attention, open monitoring and automatic self-transcending: Categories to organize meditations from Vedic, Buddhist and Chinese traditions. *Consciousness and Cognition, Volume 19*, Issue 4, December 2010, Pages 1110–1118, doi:10.1016/j.concog.2010.01.007.

20. Lutz, Antoine; Greischar, Lawrence L; Rawlings, Nancy B; Ricard, Matthieu; Davidson, Richard J (2004), Long-term Meditators Self-induce High-amplitude Gamma Synchrony During Mental Practice. *Proceedings of the National Academy of Sciences 101* (46) 16369-16373; DOI: 10.1073/pnas.0407401101

21. Travis, Fred & Shear, Jonathan (2010). Focused Attention, Open Monitoring and Automatic Self-transcending: Categories to Organize Meditations from Vedic, Buddhist and Chinese traditions. *Consciousness and Cognition, Volume 19*, Issue 4, December 2010, Pages 1110–1118, doi:10.1016/j.concog.2010.01.007

22. Lutz, A., Dunne, J.D., & Davidson, R.J. (2007). *Meditation and the Neuroscience of Consciousness*. Cambridge University Press. doi: https://doi.org/10.1017/CBO9780511816789.020

23. Tarrant, Jeff. (2017)., *Meditation Interventions to Rewire the Brain: Integrating Neuroscience Strategies for ADHD, Anxiety, Depression & PTSD*. WI: PESI Publishing & Media. p.11.

THE HEALING AWARENESS OF MINDFULNESS

1. Segal, Zindel V; Williams, Mark; Teasdale, John (2018)., *Mindfulness-Based Cognitive Therapy for Depression*. New York: The Guilford Press.

2. Kabat-Zinn, J. (2018)., *The Healing Power of Mindfulness – A New Way of Being*. New York: Hachette books.

3. Greenland, Susan K, (2010)., *The Mindful Child – How to Help Your Kid Manage Stress and Become Happier, Kinder, and More Compassionate*. New York: A Division of Simon & Schuster.

4. Schoeberlein David, Deborah & Sheth, Suki., (2009), *Mindful Teaching and Teaching Mindfulness: A Guide for Anyone Who Teaches Anything*: Massachusetts: Wisdom.

5. Ryan, Tim., (2012)., *A Mindful Nation.*, New York: Hay House Inc.

6. Moss, F., Ward, L. M., & Sannita, W. G. (2004)., *Stochastic resonance and sensory information processing: A tutorial and review of application. Clinical Neurophysiology, 115*(2), 267–281. https://doi.org/10.1016/j.clinph. 2003.09.014

7. Dias, R., Robbins, T. W., & Roberts, A. C. (1996)., *Dissociation in the prefrontal cortex of affective and attentional shifts. Nature, 380*(6569), 69-72. doi:http://dx.doi.org.du.idm.oclc. org/10.1038/380069a0.

8. Terayama, Yasuo & Meyer, John & Kawamura, Jun & Weathers, Susan. (1991)., *Role of Thalamus and White Matter in Cognitive Outcome After Head Injury. Journal of Cerebral Blood Flow and Metabolism: Official Journal of the International Society of Cerebral Blood Flow and Metabolism. 11.* 852-60. 10.1038/jcbfm.1991.145.

9. Romanski, LM and LeDoux, JE (1992)., *Equipotentiality of thalamo-amygdala and thalamo-cortico-amygdala circuits in auditory fear conditioning. Journal of Neuroscience 12* (11) 4501-4509; DOI: https://doi.org/10.1523/ JNEUROSCI.12-11-04501.1992

10. Buzsaki, G. (2011). Hippocampus. *Scholarpedia*, 6(1), 1468.

11. Frankl, Viktor E. (2006)., *Man's Search for Meaning*. MA: Boston, Beacon Press.

12. Kessler RC, Sonnega A, Bromet E, Hughes M, Nelson CB, (1995)., Posttraumatic Stress Disorder in the National Comorbidity Survey. *Arch Gen Psychiatry.* *52*(12):1048–1060. doi:10.1001/archpsyc.1995.03950240066012.

13. Brown, K. W., & Ryan, R. M. (2003)., *The Benefits of Being Present: Mindfulness and its role in psychological well-being. Journal of Personality and Social Psychology, 84*(4), 822–848.

14. Thera, Nyanaponika A. (1998)., *The Heart of Buddhist Meditation: A Handbook of Mental Training Based on the Buddha's Way of Mindfulness*. Sri Lanka: Kandy, Buddhist Puclication Society. p.45.

15. Thera, Nyanaponika A. (1998)., *The Heart of Buddhist Meditation: A Handbook of Mental Training Based on the Buddha's Way of Mindfulness*. Sri Lanka: Kandy, Buddhist Puclication Society.

16. Thera, Nyanaponika A. (1998)., *The Heart of Buddhist Meditation: A Handbook of Mental Training Based on the Buddha's Way of Mindfulness*. Sri Lanka: Kandy, Buddhist Puclication Society. p. 24.

17. Goleman, Daniel. (2005)., *Emotional Intelligence: Why It Can Matter More Than IQ*. New York: Bantam Books.

18. Nhat Hanh, T. (2006)., *Understanding Our Mind.*, CA: Berkeley, Parallax Press. p.25.

19. American Foundation for Suicide Prevention (2020), *Suicide Statistics.*, Retrieved from: https://afsp.org/about-suicide/suicide-statistics/

20. Maples, Cheri (2017), *Mindfulness and the Police.*, Retrieved from: https://static1.squarespace.com/static/55beacc8e4b0c17151842dbc/t/5984d3ae914e6b93fcd

8222f/1501877169985/MB74-Cheri-Maples-Mindfulness-Police-final-PDF.pdf

1. Rahula, Walpola. (1974)., *What the Buddha Taught.* New York: Grove Press. p. 46.

THE ROLE OF MINDFULNESS IN EDUCATION

. Sheinman, Nimrod and Hadar, Linor L. (2017)., *Mindfulness in Education – As a Whole School Approach: Principles, Insights, and Outcomes.* Cambridge Scholars Publishing, pp.77-102.

2. Sheinman, Nimrod and Hadar, Linor L, (2017), *Mindfulness in Education – As a Whole School Approach: Principles, Insights, and Outcomes.* Cambridge Scholars Publishing, pp.77-102.

3. Saltzman, Amy (2014)., *A Still Quiet Place: A Mindfulness Program for Teaching Children and Adolescents to Ease Stress and Difficult Emotions.* CA: Oakland, New Harbinge Publications, Inc.

4. Sheinman, Nimrod and Hadar, Linor L, (2017), *Mindfulness in Education – As a Whole School Approach: Principles, Insights, and Outcomes. Cambridge Scholars Publishing*, pp.77-102.

5. Wu, H., Garza, E., & Guzman, N. (2015). International Student's challenge and adjustment to college. *Education Research International*, doi:10.1155/2015/202753.

6. Kwadzo, M. (2014). International Students' Experience of Studying and Working at a Northeastern Public University in the US. *Journal of International Students, 4*(3), 279-291.

7. Eva, Amy (2019). *How Colleges Today Are Supporting Student Mental Health*, Retrieved from: https://greatergood.berkeley.edu/article/item/how_colleges_today_are_supporting_student_menta health

8. The University of Virginia (UV), *Research Finds Suspending Students, In or Out of School, is Problematic (2017, Oct 13). US Fed News Service, Including US State News.*

234 | ENDNOTES

Retrieved from https://search-proquest-com.du.idm.oclc.org/docview/1950404512?accountid=14608

9. Lynch, David (2019), *Healing Traumatic Stress and Raising Performance in At-risk Populations*: Retrieved from: https://www.davidlynchfoundation.org/schools.html#video=GCqmFpKiLD

10. Safran, J., and R. Reading. (2008). Mindfulness, metacommunication and affect regulation in psychoanalytic treatment. In Mindfulness and Psychotherapy, edited by C. Germer., R. Siegal, and P. Fulton. New York: Guildford.

11. The Satipatthana Sutta – the Discourse on the Foundations of Mindfulness, is generally regarded as the canonical Buddhist text with the fullest instructions on the system of meditation unique to the Buddha's own dispensation.

12. Bhikkhu Bodhi. (2011)., What does mindfulness really mean? A canonical perspective, *Contemporary Buddhism*, 12:1, 19-39, DOI: 10.1080/14639947.2011.564813

13. Oxford Mindfulness Center, (2019), Retrieved from: http://oxfordmindfulness.org/

14. Report by the Mindfulness All-Party Parliamentary Group (MAPPG), (2015). Mindfulness Nation UK.

15. Oxford Mindfulness Center, (2019), Retrieved from: http://oxfordmindfulness.org/

16. Nhat Hanh, Thich (2002), *Understanding Our Mind: 50 Verses on Buddhist Psychology*. California: Berkeley.

17. Leonidas, Leonardo L. (2019) *The Brain and Meditation in School*, Retrieved from: https://opinion.inquirer.net/67441/the-brain-and-meditation-in-school

18. Kabat-Zinn, Jon. (2005)., *Coming to Our Senses: Healing Ourselves and the World Through Mindfulness*, New York: Hachette.

19. Kabat-Zinn, Jon. (2005)., *Coming to Our Senses: Healing Ourselves and the World Through Mindfulness*, New York: Hachette.

20. Khoury B, Lecomte T, Fortin G, Masse M, Therien P, Bouchard V, Chapleau MA, Paquin K, Hofmann S.G., (2013)., Mindfulness-based therapy: A comprehensive meta-analysis. *Clinical Psychology Review, 33*, 763-771.

21. Chiesa, Alberto and Serretti, Alessandro. (2009)., Mindfulness-Based Stress Reduction for Stress Management in Healthy People: A Review and Meta-Analysis. *The Journal of Alternative and Complementary Medicine*, Vol. 15, No. 5. 593-600.

22. Sedlmeier P1, Eberth J, Schwarz M, Zimmermann D, Haarig F, Jaeger S, Kunze S. (2012)., The psychological effects of meditation: a meta-analysis. *Psychol Bull, 138*(6):1139-71.

23. Skinner, Ellen; Roeser, Robert; Beers, Jeffry; Jennings, Patricia. (2012)., Mindfulness Training and Teachers' Professional Development: An Emerging Area of Research and Practice. *Child Development Perspectives, 6*, 167-173.

24. Jennings, Patricia A, DeMauroAnthony A., et al. (2019)., *The Mindful School: Transforming School Culture through Mindfulness and Compassion*, New York: The Guiford Press.

25. Jennings, Patricia A, DeMauroAnthony A., et al. (2019)., *The Mindful School: Transforming School Culture through Mindfulness and Compas*sion, New York: The Guiford Press.

26. Jennings, Patricia A, DeMauroAnthony A., et al. (2019)., *The Mindful School: Transforming School Culture through Mindfulness and Compassion*, New York: The Guiford Press.

27. Jennings, P. A., Brown, J. L., Frank, J. L., Doyle, S., Oh, Y., Davis, R., Rasheed, D., DeWeese, A., DeMauro, A. A., Cham, H., & Greenberg, M. T. (2017, February 13). Impacts of the CARE for Teachers Program on Teachers' Social and Emotional Competence and Classroom Interactions. *Journal*

of Educational Psychology. Advance online publication. http://dx.doi.org/10.1037/edu0000187.

28. Roeser, R. W., Skinner, E., Beers, J., & Jennings, P. A. (2012). Mindfulness training and teachers' professional development: An emerging area of research and practice. *Child Development Perspectives, 6*(2), 167-173.

29. Meiklejohn, John; Phillips, Catherine; Freedman, M. Lee; Griffin, Mary Lee, Biegel, Gina; Roach, Andy; Frank, Jenny, Burke, Christine, Laura; Pinger, et al. (2012) Integrating Mindfulness Training into K-12 Education: Fostering the Resilience of Teachers and Students. *Mindfulness, 3*, 291-307.

30. Jennings, Patricia A. (2018). *The Trauma-Sensitive Classroom: Building Resilience with Compassionate Teaching*. New York: Norton.

31. Lynch, David. (2020)., *The Quiet Time Changes Lives*. Retrieved from: https://www.davidlynchfoundation.org/

32. Lynch, David. (2020)., *The Quiet Time Changes Lives*. Retrieved from: https://www.davidlynchfoundation.org/

33. Jennings, Patricia A. and Daniel, Siegel (2015), *Mindfulness for Teachers: Simple Skills for Peace and Productivity in the Classroom*. New York: Norton & Company.

34. Lynch, David. (2020)., *The Quiet Time Changes Lives*. Retrieved from: https://www.davidlynchfoundation.org/

35. Lynch, David (2020)., *The Quiet Time Changes Lives*. Retrieved from: https://www.davidlynchfoundation.org/

36. Lynch, David (2020)., *The Quiet Time Changes Lives*. Retrieved from: https://www.davidlynchfoundation.org/

37. Report by the Mindfulness All-Party Parliamentary Group (MAPPG), (2015). UK: Mindfulness Nation UK.

38. Mindfulness in School, (2019)., Ten Reasons to Bring Meditation to Your School., Retrieved from: http://www.meditationinschools.org/2013/06/27/10-reasons-to-bring-meditation-to-your-school/

39. Fletcher, Emily (2019)., Why Meditation Is The One Tool All Our Kids Need In Their Toolbox. Retrieved from: https://www.huffpost.com/entry/why-meditation-is-the-one_b_14521654

40. Report by the Mindfulness All-Party Parliamentary Group (MAPPG), (2015). Mindfulness Nation UK.

41. Report by the Mindfulness All-Party Parliamentary Group (MAPPG), (2015). Mindfulness Nation UK.

42. Association for mindfulness in Education. Retrieved from: http://www.mindfuleducation.org/

43. Calmer Choice. Retrieved from: https://calmerchoice.org/

44. Care for Teachers. Retrieved from: https://createforeducation.org/

45. Compassionate schools project. Retrieved from: https://www.compassionschools.org/

46. Cultivating Awareness and Resilience in Education. Retrieved from: https://createforeducation.org/care/

47. Inner explorer. Retrieved from: https://innerexplorer.org

48. Inner Kids. Retrieved from: https://www.susankaisergreenland.com/inner-kids-model

49. Inner Resilience. Retrieved from: https://lindalantieri.org/the-inner-resilience-program/

50. Inward Bound Mindfulness Education. Retrieved from: https://ibme.com/

51. Leaning to Breathe. Retrieved from: https://learning2breathe.org/

52. See Mindful Life Project. Retrieved from: http://mindfullifeproject.org/

53. Mind with Heart Mind. Retrieved from: https://www.mindwithheart.org/

54. Mindful Schools. Retrieved from: https://www.mindfulschools.org/about/

55. Mindfulness-based Kindness Curriculum. Retrieved from: https://centerhealthyminds.org/join-the-movement/sign-up-to-receive-the-kindness-curriculum

56. Mindfulness Everyday. Retrieved from: https://www.mindfulnesseveryday.org/

57. Mindfulness in Schools Project. Retrieved from: https://mindfulnessinschools.org/

58. MindUP. Retrieved from: https://mindup.org/

59. Peace in Schools. Retrieved from: https://www.peaceinschools.org/

60. Still Quiet Place. Retrieved from: http://www.stillquietplace.com/

61. Stressed Teens. Retrieved from: https://www.stressedteens.com/

62. Youth Mindfulness. Retrieved from: https://youthmindfulness.org/

63. Wake Up Schools. Retrieved from: https://wakeupschools.org/

64. Report by the Mindfulness All-Party Parliamentary Group (MAPPG), (2015). Mindfulness Nation UK.

65. Report by the Mindfulness All-Party Parliamentary Group (MAPPG), (2015). Mindfulness Nation UK.

66. Nhat Hanh, T and Weare, Katherine. (2017)., *Happy Teachers Change the World: A Guide for Cultivating Mindfulness in Education*. California: Berkeley, p. 195.

67. Nhat Hanh, T and Weare, Katherine. (2017)., *Happy Teachers Change the World: A Guide for Cultivating Mindfulness in Education*. California: Berkeley.

68. Rossi, AnneMarie. (2015)., *Why Aren't We Teaching You Mindfulness*, TEDxYouth@MileHigh, Retrieved from: https://www.youtube.com/watch?v=-yJPcdiLEkI

69. Jennings, Patricia A, DeMauroAnthony A., et al. (2019)., *The Mindful School: Transforming School Culture through Mindfulness and Compassion*. New York: The Guiford Press.

70. Jennings, Patricia A, DeMauroAnthony A., et al. (2019)., *The Mindful School: Transforming School Culture through Mindfulness and Compassion*. New York: The Guiford Press.

71. Jennings, Patricia A, DeMauroAnthony A., et al. (2019)., *The Mindful School: Transforming School Culture through Mindfulness and Compassion*. New York: The Guiford Press.

72. Ditrich, Lovegrove, Wiles. (2017)., *Mindfulness and education: Research and practice.*, Cambridge Scholars Publishing. p.77.

MINDFUL LEADERSHI

1. William Arthur Ward (1921 – 1994) was a writer and teacher. He often quoted writers of inspirational maxims. More than 100 articles, poems, and meditations written by Ward were published.

2. Lesser, Marc (2019). *Seven Practices of a Mindful Leader*: California: New World Library.

3. Jon Kabat-Zinn introduced his program of Mindfulness-Based Stress Reduction (MBSR) at the University of Massachusetts Medical Center. This program applied mindfulness techniques to reduce pain and stress has been adopted by hundreds of medical centers, hospitals and clinics around the world.

4. Gonzalez, Maria (2012)., *Mindful Leadership – The 9 Ways to Self-Awareness, Transforming Yourself, and Inspiring Others*: Canada: Jossey-Bass.

5. Zen Master Thich Nhat Hanh talked at Google 2012, link here.

6. Dr. Jon Kabat-Zinn talked at Google 2007, link here.

7. See website: https://siyli.org/about

8. McIntyre Miller, W. and Green, Zachary G. (2015)., *An integral perspective of peace leadership. Integral Leadership*

Review 15(2). http://integralleadershipreview.com/12903-47-an-integral-perspective-of-peace-leadership/

9. Goleman, Daniel. (2005)., *Emotional Intelligence: Why It Can Matter More Than IQ*., New York: Bantam, p. 43-44.

10. Gonzalez, Maria. (2012)., *Mindful Leadership – The 9 Ways to Self-Awareness, Transforming Yourself, and Inspiring Others*: Canada: Jossey-Bass.

11. Lesser, Marc. (2019)., *Seven Practices of a Mindful Leader*. California: New World Library.

12. Hanson, Rick. (2009)., *Buddha's Brain – The Practical Neuroscience of Happiness, Love & Wisdom*. CA: New Harbinger Publications, Inc.

13. Gonzalez, Maria. (2012)., *Mindful Leadership – The 9 Ways to Self-Awareness, Transforming Yourself, and Inspiring Others*. Canada: Jossey-Bass.

PRACTICE MINDFULNESS IN PRISON

1. Whitney, Kobai S. (2017)., *Sitting Inside – Buddhist Practice in America's Prisons*. MA: Deerfield, Prison Dharma Network.

2. Lozoff, Bo. (1998)., *We're All Doing Time: A Guide to Getting Free New*. NC: Durham. Human Kindness Foundation

3. David Lynch Foundation. (2020)., Retrieved from: https://www.davidlynchfoundation.org/prisons.html

4. Whitney, Kobai S. (2017)., *Sitting Inside – Buddhist Practice in America's Prisons*. MA: Deerfield, Prison Dharma Network.

5. Whitney, Kobai S. (2017)., *Sitting Inside – Buddhist Practice in America's Prisons*. MA: Deerfield, Prison Dharma Network

6. See the Religious Liberty Protection Act content at: https://www.justice.gov/crt/page/file/1006786/download

7. Reverend Kobai Scott Whiney is the Most Venerable Thich Thien An's student.

8. While the principal characters in the story have been renamed for anonymity, the content of the story remains unchanged

9. These mindfulness exercises are from Nhat Hanh, Thich (2009)., *The Blooming of a Lotus – Guided Meditation for Achieving the Miracle of Mindfulness*. MA: Boston, Beacon Press.

10. Nhat Hanh, T. (2000)., *The Part of Emancipation*. CA: Berkeley, Parallax Press. p. 222.

11. See, Nhat Hanh, Thich (2003)., *Interbeing, Full Circle Publishing*. CA: Berkeley, Parallax Press.

12. Nhat Hanh, Thich, (2006)., *Understanding Our Mind*. CA: Berkeley, Parallax Press.

13. Bhikkhu Nanamoli, Bhikkhu Bodhi Translators, (1995)., *The Middle Length Discourses of the Buddha: A Translation of the Majjhima Nikaya (The Teachings of the Buddha)*; MA: Boston, Wisdom Publications. p. 710.

14. David Lynch Foundation (2020)., Retrieved from: https://www.davidlynchfoundation.org/prisons.html

15. Kabat-Zinn, Jon, (2005)., *Wherever You Go There You Are – Mindfulness Meditation in Everyday Life*. New York: Hyperion.

16. David Lynch Foundation (2020)., Retrieved from: https://www.davidlynchfoundation.org/prisons.html

METHOD OF MINDFUL BREATHING PRACTICE

1. Bhikkhu Nanamoli, Bhikkhu Bodhi Translators, (1995)., *The Middle Length Discourses of the Buddha: A Translation of the Majjhima Nikaya (The Teachings of the Buddha)*; MA: Boston, Wisdom Publications. p.. 943.

2. Bhikkhu Nanamoli, Bhikkhu Bodhi Translators, (1995)., *The Middle Length Discourses of the Buddha: A Translation of the Majjhima Nikaya (The Teachings of the Buddha)*; MA: Boston, Wisdom Publications. p. 944.

3. Bhikkhu Nanamoli, Bhikkhu Bodhi Translators, (1995)., *The Middle Length Discourses of the Buddha: A Translation of the Majjhima Nikaya (The Teachings of the Buddha)*; MA: Boston, Wisdom Publications. p. 944.

4. Bhikkhu Nanamoli, Bhikkhu Bodhi Translators, (1995)., *The Middle Length Discourses of the Buddha: A Translation of the Majjhima Nikaya (The Teachings of the Buddha)*; MA: Boston, Wisdom Publications. p. 944.

5. Bhikkhu Nanamoli, Bhikkhu Bodhi Translators, (1995)., *The Middle Length Discourses of the Buddha: A Translation of the Majjhima Nikaya (The Teachings of the Buddha)*; MA: Boston, Wisdom Publications. p. 943.

6. Bhikkhu Nanamoli, Bhikkhu Bodhi Translators, (1995)., *The Middle Length Discourses of the Buddha: A Translation of the Majjhima Nikaya (The Teachings of the Buddha)*; MA: Boston, Wisdom Publications. p. 944.

7. Bhikkhu Nanamoli, Bhikkhu Bodhi Translators, (1995)., *The Middle Length Discourses of the Buddha: A Translation of the Majjhima Nikaya (The Teachings of the Buddha)*; MA: Boston, Wisdom Publications. p. 944.

8. Gunaratana, Bhante. (2012)., *The Foundation of Mindfulness in Plain English*. MA: Boston, Wisdom Publications.

9. Nhat Hanh, T. (2008)., *Breathe, You are alive*. CA: Berkeley, Parallax Press. p. 91.

10. Walshe, Maurice & Thera, Sumedho, (1995)., *The Long Discourses of the Buddha: A Translation of the Digha Nikaya (The Teachings of the Buddha* MA: Boston, Wisdom Publications. p.270.

11. Walshe, Maurice & Thera, Sumedho, (1995)., *The Long Discourses of the Buddha: A Translation of the Digha Nikaya (The Teachings of the Buddha)*. MA: Boston, Wisdom Publications. p.271.

REFERENCES

1. American Foundation for Suicide Prevention (2020), Suicide Statistics. Retrieved from: https://afsp.org/about-suicide/suicide-statistics/

2. Bas Verplanken (2008). *The Psychology of Habit, Theory, Mechanisms, Change, and Contexts.* Switzerland: Springer Nature.

3. Bergson, Henri., (1998)., *Evolution Creative*, Dover Publication, inc., New York: Mineole.

4. Bhikkhu Nanamoli & Bhikkhu Bodhi Translators, (1995)., *The Middle Length Discourses of the Buddha: A Translation of the Majjhima Nikaya (The Teachings of the Buddha)*; No. 118 – Anapanasati Sutta: Mindfulness of Breathing; Wisdom Publications. Boston: Massachusetts.

5. Broderick, Patricia C & Kabat-Zinn, Myla (2013)., *Learning to Breathe: A Mindfulness*

Curriculum for Adolescents to Cultivate Emotion Regulation, Attention, and Performance. CA: New Harbinger Publication

6. Brown, K. W., & Ryan, R. M. (2003). The Benefits of Being Present: Mindfulness and its role in psychological well-being. *Journal of Personality and Social Psychology, 84*(4), 822–848.

7. Buddhaghosa Bhadantacariya (Author), Bhikkhu Ñanamoli (Translator) (1995)., *The Path of Purification: Visuddhimagga.* Buddhist Publication Society. Sri Lanka: Kandy.

8. Buzsaki, G. (2011). Hippocampus. *Scholarpedia, 6*(1), 1468.

9. Calmer Choice, (2020). Retrieved from: https://calmerchoice.org/

10. Care for Teachers, (2020). Retrieved from: https://createforeducation.org/

11. Chiesa, Alberto and Serretti, Alessandro (2009). Mindfulness-Based Stress Reduction for Stress Management in Healthy People: A Review and Meta-Analysis. *The Journal of Alternative and Complementary Medicine*, Vol. 15, No. 5. 593-600.

12. Compassionate Schools Project, (2020). Retrieved from: https://www.compassionschools.org/

13. Cultivating Awareness and Resilience in Education, (2020). Retrieved from: https://createforeducation.org/care/

14. Dalai Lama, (2005)., *The Universe in A Single Atom: The Convergence of Science and Spirituality.* Harmony: Random House.

15. Dalai Lama, (2014)., *Commentary on The Thirty-Seven Practices of a Bodhisattva.* Library of Tibetan Works and Archives: Ltwa

16. David Lynch Foundation (2020)., Retrieved from: https://www.davidlynchfoundation.org/prisons.html

17. Dias, R., Robbins, T. W., & Roberts, A. C. (1996). Dissociation in the prefrontal cortex of affective and attentional shifts. *Nature, 380*(6569), 69-72. doi:http://dx.doi.org.du.idm.oclc.org/10.1038/380069a0

18. Ditrich, Lovegrove, Wiles, (2017). *Mindfulness and Education: Research and Practice.,* Cambridge Scholars Publishing.

19. Dunn, B.R., Hartigan, J.A. & Mikulas, W.L. (1999)., Concentration and Mindfulness Meditations: Unique Forms of Consciousness? *Applied Psychophysiology and Biofeedback.* 24(3): 147-165. https://doi.org/10.1023/A:1023498629385

20. Eva, Amy (2020). How Colleges Today Are Supporting Student Mental Health, Retrieved from: https://greatergood.berkeley.edu/article/item/how_colleges_today_are_supporting_student_menta health

21. Fletcher, Emily (2020)., *Why Meditation Is The One Tool All Our Kids Need In Their Toolbox.* Retrieved from: https://www.huffpost.com/entry/why-meditation-is-the-one_b_14521654

22. Frankl, Viktor E. (2006). *Man's Search for Meaning.* Boston, MA: Beacon Press. (Between stimulus and response, there is a space. In that space is our power to choose our response. In our response lies our growth and our freedom).

23. Goleman, Daniel, (2005)., *Emotional Intelligence: Why It Can Matter More Than IQ.* New York: Bantam Books.

24. Gonzalez, Maria (2012)., *Mindful Leadership – The 9 Ways to Self-Awareness, Transforming*

Yourself, and Inspiring Others: Canada: Jossey-Bass.

25. Greenland, Susan K, (2010)., *The Mindful Child – How to Help Your Kid Manage Stress and Become Happier, Kinder, and More Compassionate.* New York: A Division of Simon & Schuster.

26. Gunaratana, Bhante, (2012)., *The Foundation of Mindfulness in Plain English.* MA: Somerville, Wisdom Publications.

27. Gunaratana, Bhante, (2019)., *Eight Mindful Steps to Happiness: Walking the Buddha's Path.* MA: Somerville, Wisdom Publications.

28. Hanson, Rick (2009), *Buddha's Brain – The Practical Neuroscience of Happiness, Love & Wisdom.* CA: New Harbinger Publications, Inc.

29. Inanaga, Kazutoyo, (1998)., Frontal midline theta rhythm and mental activity. *Psychiatry Clin Neurosci. 52*(6):555-66.

30. Inner Explorer, (2020)., Retrieved from: https://innerexplorer.org/

31. Inner Kids, (2020)., Retrieved from: https://www.susankaisergreenland.com/inner-kids-model

32. Inner Resilience (2020)., Retrieved from: https://lindalantieri.org/the-inner-resilience-program/

33. Inward Bound Mindfulness Education, (2020)., Retrieved from: https://ibme.com/

34. Jennings, P. A., Brown, J. L., Frank, J. L., Doyle, S., Oh, Y., Davis, R.,... Greenberg, M. T. (2017). Impacts of the CARE for Teachers program on teachers' social and emotional competence and classroom interactions. *Journal of Educational Psychology, 109*(7), 1010-1028.

35. Jennings, P. A., Brown, J. L., Frank, J. L., Doyle, S., Oh, Y., Davis, R., Rasheed, D., DeWeese, A., DeMauro, A. A., Cham, H., & Greenberg, M. T. (2017, February 13). Impacts of the CARE for Teachers Program on Teachers' Social and Emotional Competence and Classroom Interactions. *Journal of Educational Psychology.* Advance online publication. http://dx.doi.org/10.1037/edu0000187

36. Jennings, Patricia A (2018). *The Trauma-Sensitive Classroom: Building Resilience with Compassionate Teaching.* New York: Norton.

37. Jennings, Patricia A, DeMauroAnthony A., et al. (2019), *The Mindful School: Transforming School Culture through Mindfulness and Compassion,* New York: The Guiford Press.

38. Jennings, Patricia A. (2015), *Mindfulness for Teachers: Simple Skills for Peace and Productivity in the Classroom*. New York: Norton & Company

39. Jennings, Patricia A., and Greenberg, Mark T. (2009) The Prosocial Classroom: Teacher Social and Emotional Competence in Relation to Student and Classroom Outcomes. *Review of Educational Research, 79*, 491-525.

40. K.R. Norman (2004), *The Word of the Doctrine*, The Pāli Text Society.

41. Kabat-Zinn, J. (2013). *Full Catastrophe Living: Using the Wisdom of Your Body and Mind to Face Stress, Pain, and Illness*, New York: Bantam.

42. Kabat-Zinn, Jon, (2005)., *Wherever You Go There You Are – Mindfulness Meditation in Everyday Life*. New York: Hyperion.

43. Kabat-Zinn, Jon, (2018)., *The Healing Power of Mindfulness – A New Way of Being.*, Boston: New York.

44. Kabat-Zinn, Jon. (2005), *Coming to Our Senses: Healing Ourselves and the World Through Mindfulness*, New York: Hachette.

45. Kelley Raab (2014)., Mindfulness, Self-Compassion, and Empathy Among Health Care

Professionals: A Review of the Literature, *Journal of Health Care Chaplaincy, 20*:3, 95-108, DOI: 10.1080/08854726.2014.913876

46. Kessler RC, Sonnega A, Bromet E, Hughes M, Nelson CB, (1995). Posttraumatic Stress Disorder in the National Comorbidity Survey. *Arch Gen Psychiatry. 52*(12):1048–1060. doi:10.1001/archpsyc.1995.03950240066012.

47. Khoury B, Lecomte T, Fortin G, Masse M, Therien P, Bouchard V, Chapleau MA, Paquin K, Hofmann S.G., (2013). Mindfulness-based therapy: A comprehensive meta-analysis. *Clinical Psychology Review, 33*, 763-771.

48. Kwadzo, M. (2014). International Students' Experience of Studying and Working at a Northeastern Public University in the US. *Journal of International Students, 4*(3), 279-291.

49. Learning to Breathe., (2020)., Retrieved from: https://learning2breathe.org/

50. Lehrhaupt, L., & Meibert, P, (2017). *Mindfulness-Based Stress Reduction – The MBSR Program for Enhancing Health and Vitality*, Novato, California: New World Library.

51. Leonidas, Leonardo L. (2020) *The Brain and Meditation in School*, Retrieved from: https://

opinion.inquirer.net/67441/the-brain-and-
meditation-in-school

52. Lesser, Marc (2019). *Seven Practices of a Mindful Leader*: California, New World Library.

53. Linden, David J. (2007). *The Accidental Mind: How Brain Evolution Has Given Us Love, Memory, Dreams, and God*. Cambridge, MA: The Belknap Press of Harvard University Press.

54. Lozoff, Bo, (1998)., *We're All Doing Time: A Guide to Getting Free New*. NC: Durham. Human Kindness Foundation.

55. Lutz, A., Dunne, J.D., & Davidson, R.J. (2007). *Meditation and the Neuroscience of Consciousness*. Cambridge University Press. doi: https://doi.org/10.1017/CBO9780511816789.020

56. Lutz, Antoine; Greischar, Lawrence L; Rawlings, Nancy B; Ricard, Matthieu; Davidson, Richard J (2004), Long-term Meditators Self-induce High-amplitude Gamma Synchrony During Mental Practice. *Proceedings of the National Academy of Sciences 101* (46) 16369-16373; DOI: 10.1073/pnas.0407401101

57. Lynch, David (2020)., *The Quiet Time Changes Lives*. Retrieved from: https://www.davidlynchfoundation.org/

58. Mahasi Sayadaw (Author), Maung Tha Noe (Translator), (1991)., *Fundamentals of Vipassana Meditation*, New Jersey: Dhammachakka Meditation Center.

59. Maples, Cheri (2017), *Mindfulness and the Police.*, Retrieved from: https://static1.squarespace.com/ static/55beacc8e4b0c17151842dbc/t/5984d3ae9 14e6b93fcd8222f/1501877169985/MB74-Cheri-Maples-Mindfulness-Police-final-PDF.pdf

60. McIntyre Miller, W. and Green, Zachary G., (2015). *An integral perspective of peace leadership. Integral Leadership Review 15*(2). http://integralleadershipreview.com/12903-47-an-integral-perspective-of-peace-leadership/

61. Meiklejohn, John; Phillips, Catherine; Freedman, M. Lee; Griffin, Mary Lee, Biegel, Gina; Roach, Andy; Frank, Jenny, Burke, Christine, Laura; Pinger, et al. (2012) Integrating Mindfulness Training into K-12 Education: Fostering the Resilience of Teachers and Students. *Mindfulness, 3*, 291-307.

62. Mind with Heart Mind., (2020). Retried from: https://www.mindwithheart.org/

63. Mindful Life Project, (2020). Retried from: http://mindfullifeproject.org/

64. Mindful School., (2020). Retrieved from: https://www.mindfulschools.org/

65. Mindfulness Everyday, (2020). Retrieved from: https://www.mindfulnesseveryday.org/

66. Mindfulness in School Project., (2020). Retrieved from: https://mindfulnessinschools.org/

67. Mindfulness in School, (2020)., *Ten Reasons to Bring Meditation to Your School*., Retrieved from: http://www.meditationinschools.org/2013/06/27/10-reasons-to-bring-meditation-to-your-school/

68. Mindfulness-based Kindness Curriculum., (2020). Retrieved from: https://centerhealthyminds.org/join-the-movement/sign-up-to-receive-the-kindness-curriculum

69. MindUP., (2020). Retrieved from: https://mindup.org/

70. Moss, F., Ward, L. M., & Sannita, W. G. (2004). Stochastic resonance and sensory information processing: A tutorial and review of application. *Clinical Neurophysiology, 115*(2), 267–281. https://doi.org/10.1016/j.clinph.2003.09.014

71. Nhat Hanh, T and Weare, Katherine (2017)., *Happy Teachers Change the World: A Guide for*

Cultivating Mindfulness in Education. California: Berkeley.

72. Nhat Hanh, Thich (1999)., *Call me by my True names*, CA: Berkeley, Parallax Press.

73. Nhat Hanh, Thich (2002), *Understanding Our Mind: 50 Verses on Buddhist Psychology*. California: Berkeley.

74. Nhat Hanh, Thich (2003)., *Interbeing*, Full Circle Publishing.

75. Nhat Hanh, Thich, (2006)., *Transformation & Healing, Sutra on the Four Establishments of Mindfulness*. CA: Berkeley, Parallax Press.

76. Nhat Hanh, Thich, (2007)., *Buddha Mind, Buddha Body – Walkinh Toward Enlightment*. CA: Berkeley, Parallax Press.

77. Nhat Hanh, Thich, (2008)., *Breathe, You are alive*. CA: Berkeley, Parallax Press.

78. Nhat Hanh, Thich, (2010)., *The Diamond That Cuts Through Illusion*. CA: Berkeley, Parallax Press.

79. Nhat Hanh, Thich, (2017)., *The Other Shore, A New Translation of the Heart Sutta with Commentaries.*, CA: Berkeley, Parallax Press.

80. Nhat Hanh, Thích., (2000). *The Part of Emancipation*. CA: Berkeley, Parallax Press.

81. Nhat Hanh, Thich., (2009). *The Blooming of a Lotus, Guided Meditation for Achieving the Miracle of Mindfulness*: MA: Boston.

82. Oxford Mindfulness Center, (2020), Retrieved from: http://oxfordmindfulness.org/

83. Peace in Schools., (2020). Retrieved from: https://www.peaceinschools.org/

84. Rahula, Walpola, (1974)., *What the Buddha Taught*, New York: Grove Press.

85. Roeser, R. W., Skinner, E., Beers, J., & Jennings, P. A. (2012). Mindfulness training and teachers' professional development: An emerging area of research and practice. Child Development Perspectives, 6(2), 167-173.

86. Romanski, LM and LeDoux, JE (1992)., Equipotentiality of thalamo-amygdala and thalamo-cortico-amygdala circuits in auditory fear conditioning. *Journal of Neuroscience 12* (11) 4501-4509; DOI: https://doi.org/10.1523/JNEUROSCI.12-11-04501.1992

87. Rossi, AnneMarie (2015), *Why Aren't We Teaching You Mindfulness*, TEDxYouth@

MileHigh, Retrieved from: https://www.youtube.com/watch?v=-yJPcdiLEkI

88. Ryan, Tim., (2012)., *A Mindful Nation.*, New York: Hay House Inc.

89. Saltzman, Amy (2014)., *A Still Quiet Place: A Mindfulness Program for Teaching Children and Adolescents to Ease Stress and Difficult Emotions.* California: New Harbinger Publications:

90. Schoeberlein David, Deborah & Sheth, Suki., (2009), *Mindful Teaching and Teaching Mindfulness: A Guide for Anyone Who Teaches Anything*: MA: Wisdom, Publications.

91. Search Inside Yourself (SIY). Retrieved from: https://siyli.org/about

92. Sedlmeier P1, Eberth J, Schwarz M, Zimmermann D, Haarig F, Jaeger S, Kunze S. (2012). The psychological effects of meditation: a meta-analysis. *Psychol Bull, 138*(6):1139-71

93. Segal, Zindel V; Williams, Mark; Teasdale, John (2018). *Mindfulness-Based Cognitive Therapy for Depression.* New York: The Guilford Press.

94. Sheinman, Nimrod and Hadar, Linor L, (2017), Mindfulness in Education – As a Whole School

Approach: Principles, Insights, and Outcomes. Cambridge Scholars Publishing, pp.77-102.

95. Siegel, Daniel (2007)., *The Mindful Brain: Reflection and Attunement in the Cultivation of Well-Being*. New York: Norton & Company.

96. Skinner, Ellen; Roeser, Robert; Beers, Jeffry; Jennings, Patricia (2012). Mindfulness Training and Teachers' Professional Development: An Emerging Area of Research and Practice. *Child Development Perspectives, 6*, 167-173.

97. Stevens, Rosemary A. and Jr. Shapiro (2017)., *Meditation: Self-regulation Strategy and Altered State of Consciousness*: New York: Routledge.

98. Still Quiet Place., (2020). Retrieved from: http://www.stillquietplace.com/

99. Streesed Teens., (2020). Retrieved from: https://www.stressedteens.com/

100. Suzuki, Shunryu (1996)., *Zen Mind, Beginner's Mind: Informal Talks on Zen Meditation and Practice*. New York: Published by Weatherhil, Inc.,

101. Tarrant, Jeff, (2017). *Meditation Interventions to Rewire the Brain: Integrating Neuroscience*

Strategies for ADHD, Anxiety, Depression & PTSD: WI: Pesi Publishing & Media,

102. Terayama, Yasuo & Meyer, John & Kawamura, Jun & Weathers, Susan. (1991). Role of Thalamus and White Matter in Cognitive Outcome After Head Injury. Journal of Cerebral Blood Flow and Metabolism: *Official Journal of the International Society of Cerebral Blood Flow and Metabolism. 11.* 852-60. 10.1038/jcbfm.1991.145.

103. The Association for Mindfulness in Education., (2020). Retrieved from: http://www. mindfuleducation.org/

104. The Mindfulness All-Party Parliamentary Group (MAPPG), (2015). *Mindfulness Nation UK.*

105. The Religious Liberty Protection Act content at: https://www.justice.gov/crt/page/file/1006786/ download

106. Thera, Nyanaponika A. (1998),. *The Heart of Buddhist Meditation: A Handbook of Mental Training Based on the Buddha's Way of Mindfulness.,* Sri Lanka: Kandy, Buddhist Puclication Society.

107. These mindfulness exercise are from Nhat Hanh, Thich (2009)., *The Blooming of a Lotus –*

Guided Meditation for Achieving the Miracle of Mindfulness. MA: Boston, Beacon Press.

108. Travis, Fred & Shear, Jonathan (2010). Focused attention, open monitoring and automatic self-transcending: Categories to organize meditations from Vedic, Buddhist and Chinese traditions. *Consciousness and Cognition, Volume 19*, Issue 4, December 2010, Pages 1110–1118, doi:10.1016/j.concog.2010.01.007.

109. Vo, Dzung X. (2015)., *The Mindful Teen: Powerful Skills to Help You Handle Stress One Moment at a Time*. CA: Instant Help.

110. Vung Q. Doan aka Minh Hai, (2018)., *Living on Happiness: A guide to practicing mindfulness in daily life*. CA: Bodhi Media.

111. Wake Up School., (2019). Retrieved from: https://wakeupschools.org/

112. Walshe, Maurice & Thera, Sumedho, (1995)., *The Long Discourses of the Buddha: A Translation of the Digha Nikaya* (*The Teachings of the Buddha*). MA: Wisdom Publications.

113. Whitney, Kobai S., (2017). *Sitting Inside – Buddhist Practice in America's Prisons*. MA: Deerfield, Prison Dhamma Network.

114. Williams, Mark & Teasdale, John (2007)., *The Mindful Way Through Depression: Freeing Yourself from Chronic Unhappiness*. New York: Guilford Press.

115. Wu, H., Garza, E., & Guzman, N. (2015). International Student's challenge and adjustment to college. *Education Research International, doi:10*.1155/2015/202753.

116. Youth Mindfulness., (2020). Retrieved from: https://youthmindfulness.org/

About the author

Vung Q Doan aka Minh Hai, graduated with a Bachelor in Buddhist Studies and a Bachelor of Psychology. He also finished a Master in Educational Psychology and is currently in a second-year students Doctor of Higher Education program. He has practiced mindful meditation and has been an avid follower of the traditional Zen Master Thich Nhat Hanh since 2003.

He is a mindfulness teacher, a translator, and a writer. He teaches mindful meditation in prison and also guides local youths in how to improve mental health problems. He wants to bring the miracle of mindfulness to achieve a happy life through mindful awareness, a practice that can be applied by anyone and anywhere.